Invisible No More

Ahelia Publishing

Helena, Montana

Invisible No More

Healing Identity: Answering the Call to Arms

Book One—Healing Relational Perspective

Jocelyn Anne Drozda

M.Ed, B.Ed

Invisible—No More
Healing Identity: Answering the Call to Arms
Book One—Healing Relational Perspective

Copyright 2018 Jocelyn Anne Drozda

All rights reserved. No part of this publication may be reproduced, stored in a retrieval system, or transmitted in any form by any process—electronic, mechanical, photocopying, recording, or otherwise—without prior written permission of the copyright owners and Ahelia Publishing, Inc. Any scanning, uploading, and distribution of this book via the Internet or any other means without the permission of the publisher is illegal and punishable by law.

Unless otherwise indicated, all Scriptures are taken from THE HOLY BIBLE, ENGLISH STANDARD VERSION (ESV): Scriptures taken from THE HOLY BIBLE, ENGLISH STANDARD VERSION ® Copyright ©2001 by Crossway, a publishing ministry of Good News Publishers. Used by permission.

Scriptures marked NLT are taken from the HOLY BIBLE, NEW LIVING TRANSLATION (NLT): Scriptures taken from the HOLY BIBLE, NEW LIVING TRANSLATION, Copyright© 1996, 2004, 2007 by Tyndale House Foundation. Used by permission of Tyndale House Publishers, Inc., Carol Stream, Illinois 60188. All rights reserved. Used by permission.

Scriptures marked NKJV are taken from the NEW KING JAMES VERSION (NKJV): Scripture taken from the NEW KING JAMES VERSION®. Copyright© 1982 by Thomas Nelson, Inc. Used by permission. All rights reserved.

ISBN# 978-1-988001-30-2

Published in the United States of America
Printed in the United States of America
www.aheliapublishing.com

AHELIA PUBLISHING, INC.

Invisible No More
Healing Identity: Answering the Call to Arms

Jocelyn was a face that I saw on a Sunday morning at church–not knowing much about her. Even though we were involved in some of the same ministries–Cleansing Stream and the Prophetic–we never knew each other. I remember the day, well not the exact day, but our Cleansing Stream team was having a prayer session at our church and I felt the Lord deposit a word for Jocelyn to me. I knew it wasn't to be given off to the side or in private, but in front of the entire team assembled–like when Samuel called David out in front of his brothers and the congregation assembled.

I don't remember the exact word that I gave, as in most instances, when God gives me a prophetic word for someone, it's left between that person and God. However, I believe that word was a time of dedication and anointing for the plans and purposes God had in store for her. I believe this very manual may have been directly or indirectly birthed from that word or confirmed what she was already feeling and what others had spoken over her. Over the years, I have been given the opportunity to speak into her life on numerous occasions and speak/confirm God's plans for Jocelyn–from opportunities for public speaking, writing books/manuals, and hosting/organizing conferences. It is awesome to see her walk in the calling God has for her. I consider it not only a privilege to be part of seeing her fulfill God's destiny, but also it's a privilege to call her a friend.

Glenn Paguyo
Prophetic Leadership Team Member
Deliverance Ministry Leadership Team Member
Harvest City Church, Canada

➤➤➤This guide can be used individually or with a partner, for small groups or Bible studies, and in large group settings. If you are interested in having Jocelyn present a seminar for your retreat or conference, please contact her at:

jdrozda@myaccess.ca

Dedicated to The Ones for whom I fight ...

So humble yourselves under the mighty power of God, and at the right time he will lift you up in honor. Give all your worries and cares to God, for he cares about you.
1 Peter 5:6-7 (NLT)

"I will set my heart and my soul to seek the Lord my God."
adapted from 1 Chronicles 22:19

Table of Contents

My Heart to Yours — Page 8

Healing Identity: Answering the Call to Arms—Introduction — Page 10

Book One—Healing Relational Perspective — Page 12

- Unit One—Walking in Invisibility — Page 15
- Unit Two—My Princess Heart — Page 35
- Unit Three—Stand up, Girl! — Page 48
- Unit Four—Steps of My Own — Page 62
- Unit Five—Linking Shields — Page 73
- Unit Six—Letting Go — Page 87
- Unit Seven—Held Accountable — Page 103

Appendix

- Prophetic Pictures — Page 118
- I am Found — Page 119
- My Outward Expressions — Page 120
- My Inward Expressions — Page 122
- My Declaration — Page 124
- My Healing Testimony — Page 125
- Prophetic Voices — Page 126
- Endnotes — Page 127
- Acknowledgments — Page 128
- Endorsements — Page 129
- Introducing Book Two—Personal Identity Restored — Page 131

My Heart to Yours

We decide who we are. We create our own identity by the beliefs we hold about ourselves—who we believe ourselves to be. We even go so far as to subconsciously structure the world around us —people we allow in our lives, decisions we make, situations we construct, so the identity we have created for ourselves remains intact and in line with the beliefs at the core of its formation. We unknowingly convince ourselves that others, and by extension, God, see us in this same light. Firmly pocketing every life situation and interaction that supports our created identity, we barely give an audible voice to those things that speak of its opposition. Yet it is in this very opposition we often find our true identity—the person who God specifically designed us to be to fulfill the unique purposes for which He created us.

It is in knowing fully who you are—who you were originally intended to be, not how you have been shaped by your life experiences, that enables you to walk in the authority allotted you by your rightful position in the Kingdom of Heaven. You are a child of the Most High God, co-heir to the throne with Christ, and a highly favored, much loved child. There are no insecurities, fears, anxieties, infirmities, or negativity in the Kingdom. Yet these very things can become the basis of our falsely created identity. You may know your identity in Christ cognitively, but until you receive it in its entirety in your heart, with all its glorious implications, you will not feel it, nor see it manifested in your life.

I came to a point in my life where I felt pushed hard up against a wall. There was no way forward, yet I could not go backward. The walls seemed to be pressing in on me from all sides, the roof collapsing, and the foundation crumbling. I had been hanging on to God with both hands for many years, going hard after my healing. I had received incredible victory over past circumstances I had faced in my life, but as the trauma was healed and the mess unraveled, I began to understand that I was not who I had believed myself to be all these years. My entire life had, instead, been built on a foundation of lies.

I was more than stunned. As layers of tangled mess were stripped away, I discovered that at the raw core of who I thought I was, what I had believed about myself, about God, how I interacted with the world, how I structured my entire life, was based on an intricate network of false beliefs—lie after lie constructed on the back of its predecessor. It was like the fabric of my very being had to be unraveled, thread by thread, until those first evil seeds planted by the enemy were exposed, so God could weave me back together into the person He intended me to be from the beginning of the ages.

This is the story of my ongoing journey of this healing of my identity—how I am answering His call to arms. As hard as it is, God has asked me to share it with you, being agonizingly transparent in the process. And I do it, in submission to the request of my Lord, knowing it will bring freedom to people, and in turn, will set me free. I am excited to sit down with you over coffee one day, and hear your story of stepping into your true identity. It is a hard journey, overwhelming at times, but a quest well worth the effort. Bring a box of tissues; chances are you'll need them. I did.

Walk in peace and joy, my friend,
Jocelyn Anne Drozda

> So shall My word be that goes forth from My mouth;
> It shall not return to Me void,
> But it shall accomplish what I please,
> And it shall prosper in the thing for which I sent it.
> Isaiah 55:11 (NKJV)

So be it, Lord …

Healing Identity: Answering the Call to Arms

Introduction

This three-part guide is not about discovering every facet of your outward identity, such as how you like your eggs, your favorite song, or how you creatively express yourself; although I have included a place for that just for fun! (Pg. 120-121) No. It is about healing your identity so you can answer the Lord's call to arms with courage, strength, and ferocity. It is about learning who you are so you can stand unwavering and steadfast in the midst of any battle or attack. It is about putting yourself into the spotlight to examine how you fit—or don't fit—into the world around you, and asking the difficult questions, stirring up, overturning those long-forgotten, deeply buried places in your heart to expose the foundation on which you have built your life.

It is about rebuilding the parts that have deteriorated along the way, or that were built with faulty construction in the first place. It is about not feeling invisible, less than, unworthy, or _____ anymore, and shedding some light on why you have felt that way, for perhaps much of your life. It is about healing, repairing, and refining some relationships … and perhaps letting go of others. It is about repentance and deeply forgiving others, forgiving yourself, forgiving God—not leaving those secret, *untouchable* areas untouched. It is about exploring the relentless, reckless love of God. Its purpose is to turn your heart inside out so those hidden, locked places can be healed from the inside out, so you can uncover and step into your original, God-given identity and purposes.

This course is about dumping all the *yuck*, the ugliness that has accumulated and has been carried in your mind and heart, sometimes for decades or even generations, to make room to carry more of Christ's character and glory. It is about letting yourself and others off the self-imposed hooks to learn to walk in freedom. It is about ripping enemy targets off your back, picking up your own weapons and learning how to fight, exchanging the darkness for light. It requires you to step up on the platform, grab the microphone, and expose the vulnerable places to bring revelation, restoration, and redemption to those tender, scarred places of your soul.

Its intent is not to bring guilt, shame, or condemnation, but to wash it out so you can stand up, step out into the light and be seen. It intends to help you discover your value so you will no longer let yourself be walked on … and no longer walk on others. It will encourage you to stand straight and tall, with your head held up, your chest out, in the confidence of the Lord, dressed in full battle armor of righteousness, and carrying your sword and shield. It will help you to see yourself as He sees you—the child of the Almighty He originally intended you to be, with all the privileges and authority this position grants you. It is about keeping your head up so the crown He has given you can stay on your head, but also knowing when to lay this very crown at His feet.

This guide delves into learning how to hear His voice so you can follow the path of gems He leaves for you with sharpness and precision, enabling you to walk in your own destiny with confidence and assurance. It is about no longer feeling invisible, unworthy, or unloved, so you can reach out, love others, and not only impact all of the people God has put in your sphere of influence, but widen it. It is time to align yourself with God's truth and His purposes for your life, so you can step into all He has for you and others through you as you answer His call to arms. It is time for your breakthrough. It is time to find your voice.

> "My sheep hear My voice, and I know them, and they follow Me.
> I give them eternal life, and they will never perish;
> and no one will snatch them out of My hand.
> My Father, who has given them to Me, is greater than all,
> and no one is able to snatch them out of My Father's hand.
> I and My Father are one."
> John 10:27-30

Book One
Healing Relational Perspective

But the Lord GOD helps me; therefore I have not been disgraced; therefore I have set my face like a flint, and I know that I shall not be put to shame. He who vindicates me is near. Who will contend with me? Let us stand up together.

Isaiah 50:7-8a

My crash course on identity was initiated by too many things coming too hard against me all at once. God allowed these very events so He could begin to root out the lies needing to be removed from my soul. It was these lies that built false perceptions and prevented me from knowing my true identity. I knew who I was supposed to be in Christ, but I also knew I wasn't that person. And I certainly did not *feel* like that person.

As I began this quest, my dear friend, Kimm Reid, prayed with me. The very next day, for five straight hours, the Lord took me through various steps of healing. The next week, another wave of torment would hit, and again I would bury myself away with the Lord, and He would expose more of the roots that had tangled themselves within me, corrupting my thinking and the understanding of my true identity. Again and again, week upon week, this would happen. Each step would bring healing and lead me closer to my original design. The waves are still coming, only they have slowed down to a trickle now. The result of this process is this guide to the healing of identity.

And it is just that—a *guide*, so please use it as so. Since the Lord works differently in each one of us, making our journeys sweetly unique, take the "scenic routes" as He directs you. Pause when you have to, and circle back around as many times as you need, as deeper layers are uncovered. This guide is more an invitation to explore, than a formula. Though some healing comes immediately, some unfolds slowly, through a fascinating process of revelation.

I have asked my friend if I could share with you the prayer she prayed over me, the one that opened this incredible door so many months ago. I have adapted her prayer so you can pray it over yourself as you begin your own precious healing journey.

Prayer:
Dear Lord, You are so good, so amazing, kind, and gracious. Thank You that You love me too much to leave me where I am. Thank You for bringing me to this place, even though it is ugly, nasty, hard, painful; it hurts.

When we are sick, we know we need to take measures to heal our body. But Lord, we can't do this on our own. So Father, thank You that You have made Your truth known; that You are just waiting to unveil my eyes to show me my actual identity, my true identity, not the identity the world sets me up to know. The world is broken and people are broken. So God, forgive me for looking to broken people to tell me who I am. They can't. But You not only can, You want to.

I pray You give me courage and strength to knock down every block I am using to barricade myself into this false identity—the things I have maybe even forgotten about, but they are still blocking. Thank You for bringing those things to remembrance. I thank You that You are the God of justice and that You'll come in and You will reign supreme. You will have Your way. You will hold accountable everyone who needs to be held accountable. I don't need to even worry about it. I can let them go. I ask You for strength and courage to forgive those who have so wounded me.

I can say, God, I am Your problem. My problem is Your problem. You have never asked me to fix my problems. You have asked me only to fix my eyes on You and trust You. So Lord, as I knock down these blocks and light begins to come in, I ask for breakthrough in this, that like Lazarus when he came out of the tomb and the death clothes were taken from him and light came in, I ask You that in a moment, my heart will open and I will see myself as You see me. And I will know in a moment my true identity; that I am not only of highest value, but God, that You have an eternity of unending, unrelenting love for me ... and that I am not invisible, or _____, but You see me and are preparing me and that changes everything.

I ask that You will gently speak to me, gently lead me and please give me experiences of Your truth. Replace all the experiences of the enemy with a double portion of experiences of You. Have people begin to come up and begin to reiterate what You are showing me. Unveil my eyes. Show me who I am. As You bring me out into the light, cause people all over the place to acknowledge me in small ways, in great ways. Open my eyes to be aware of this—that I am not invisible, unloved, or unworthy ... less than. I bind up any pride, shame, or condemnation that try to interfere with the healing of my identity.

God, I break off the lie that says I have to make myself seen. It is in Your hands, God. I am seen. I ask for freedom in this area, for experiential truth, and that You will have Your way. I pray this in Jesus' name. Amen.

—Kimm Reid

Unit One
Walking in Invisibility

Invisible. Some days, that seemed to be my middle name. Overlooked. Uninvited. Forgotten. Unchosen. (That was my favorite go-to name in my unhealthy identity.) The picture painted by the choice of negative words in my self-talk is starkly apparent. I often felt forgotten by the world, left out of society—unimportant, I did not matter.

Situation upon situation would arise that seemed to reinforce this belief I held, until it became painfully deep-seated. "I could fall off the face of the earth and no one would notice." Time and time again I spoke this lie over my life. And words have power. By the time I graduated high school, this pattern was already established in my life, and only grew more deeply entrenched in my adult world. And the enemy, always eager for a chance to kill, steal, and destroy (John 10:10), greedily latched on to the target that had been placed on my back. He relentlessly sought opportunities to reinforce my feelings of invisibility, of being unnoticed, often manifesting in absurd, yet cruel scenarios.

What was to be a photo spread in the local paper announcing I had won the juried art show, was relegated to a few lines at the back, the camera broken. Unintentionally being left off of lists, whether it be wedding invitations, emails, staff introductions or acknowledgments of gratitude became routine, rather than isolated events. I was even left uninvited to my own induction into the teaching federation! I soon became the one who took pictures of others, rather than being requested to be in them. Invitations to luncheons and events were blatantly extended to everyone in the room, except me. Often times I would *meet* the same person over and over, as they had totally forgotten they had met me several times previously. It was not an uplifting feeling as I noted how unmemorable I must be for this to happen so often, and it only cemented the belief in my heart of how unimportant I must be. In different facets of my life, decisions that concerned me were made without my input, leaving me once again feeling like I did not exist in their world.

My feelings of invisibility multiplied as I was passed over for opportunity after opportunity in which I felt more than capable. Relationally as well, I rarely felt I ever fit into society, always being at a different stage or state in life than most of my peers—constantly half a step out of sync. This only intensified my feelings of being left out—unchosen.

Unhealthy relationships into which I entered over the years did little to eradicate this false belief. They only served to expand the wounding that was already done to my heart. And they too, imprinted their harsh message onto my soul that yes, I truly was unimportant in this life. My opinion counted for nothing. I had no voice. Whatever I did, didn't matter. I did not matter.

However, throughout the years, my life on the outside would have appeared to contradict the internal struggle I continually battled. I had a very supportive family of origin, families who adopted me, and many close friends. I excelled both personally and professionally, earning many awards and commendations. I was very much a high (possibly *over*) achiever.

I became well know in my niche of the education system. As an unofficial consultant, I was often called upon by the Ministry of Education and various school divisions to deliver presentations at conferences, provincial and national alike, over a ten-year-span. I began to publish and sell teaching resources I created, to a surprisingly wide market, though they were specifically designed to meet the requirements of my own provincial curriculum. This led to the opportunity for me to write for two other publishing companies who sought me out. I also sat on many committees that had an impact on education in the province.

Yet, in spite of all this, the feeling of invisibility, though never a pervasive force, was always the underlying theme of my life, rearing its ugly head at the most awkward and inopportune times, causing a flare-up of overreaction and heartbreak. It was as though every situation which screamed, "Stand up! Be seen! You have a voice!" was minimized in my thinking, passed over without being internalized. And every circumstance where I was overlooked or unseen was magnified to the extreme.

I was finally confronted head-on with this issue of "my invisibility" when the enemy hit this same target with his fiery darts from almost every possible angle at once. Overplaying his hand, he forced me to intentionally seek the Lord to uncover why I have felt savagely tormented in this manner for so, so long. Seeking advise and prayer from a wise and trusted friend, she peeled back layers of hurt to reveal some core issues.

Hearing from the Lord, she recounted that even if God wanted to heal me right now, He couldn't, because I had *decided* I was invisible. It was a deep wound and **I had received it as my identity.** This made my present feelings of not being seen—not being important—an open door, or in other words, a target on my back, allowing the enemy to focus his relentless attacks on it. And I willingly partnered with it each time I said, "You see … I am invisible or this would not have happened," as even unintentional incidents of being overlooked (that occasionally happen to everyone in our busy society) began to reinforce my falsely constructed identity.

Each negative incident became a building block that eventually constructed a huge, immoveable fortress that surrounded me, barricading me in. Due to my experiences, my heart believed I was invisible, unimportant, unchosen. And so I was—"For as he thinks in his heart, so *is* he" (Proverbs 23:7 NKJV).

"But there are the experiences you know, and there is *the truth*, and those are not the same things," encouraged my friend. "We need to understand the truth is not necessarily what we are seeing (or believing)." What we see becomes our justification to feel the way we feel; but it also becomes the lock on the cage in which we then inhabit. And this cage keeps us from seeing ourselves as we truly are—as God sees us. It prevents us from recognizing our God-created identity. It keeps us in captivity, deterring us from holding the positional authority we have inherited as adopted children of the King, and from walking in the full destiny for which God created us.

From this conversation began an intimate journey with the Lord as He unraveled, unveiled, and healed my identity. It started with me laying down all the insidiously woven false beliefs in which I currently identified—had firmly held on to for so long. These had served to become the drawn sword fending off only the Lord Himself, and kept me from realizing and understanding who I truly was. They had become tools of the enemy, used to confuse me, bind me, contain me. I repented for holding these beliefs, as how could they have possibly been *His truth* about me? And then I asked the Almighty Lord God to open my eyes so I could see myself as He saw me ... show me through His eyes who I was ... who He really created me to be, before the beginning of time. It has been the journey of a lifetime—literally. But becoming totally undone was the only way I could be put back together with truth as the firm foundation, ready to step into all the glorious promises He has for me.

Expressions of Invisibility

These words all speak to the concept of invisibility and can be exchanged with the word *invisible* throughout the guide. At your lowest point, what is your self-talk? What is your *invisible*? Check off the words with which you identify. Record them in the box on the following page. This is where your journey begins.

- ○ hidden
- ○ disguised
- ○ imperceptible
- ○ masked
- ○ obscured
- ○ unnoticeable
- ○ unseen
- ○ veiled
- ○ imperceivable
- ○ unknown
- ○ insignificant
- ○ concealed
- ○ suppressed
- ○ underdeveloped
- ○ undeveloped
- ○ not enough
- ○ replaceable

- ○ unchosen
- ○ uninvited
- ○ forgotten
- ○ overlooked
- ○ inconsequential
- ○ irrelevant
- ○ lesser
- ○ unimportant
- ○ of no significance
- ○ inadequate
- ○ unrealized
- ○ insufficient
- ○ worthless
- ○ of no use
- ○ without value
- ○ unappreciated
- ○ unheard

- ○ rejected
- ○ inferior
- ○ useless
- ○ valueless
- ○ unworthy
- ○ wretched
- ○ less than
- ○ unqualified
- ○ unexpressed
- ○ abandoned
- ○ unloved
- ○ unlovable
- ○ not worth pursuing
- ○ silenced
- ○ not good enough
- ○ unneeded
- ○ _____

No More!

Feeling invisible extends far beyond the concept of being unseen by others, by God. It makes us feel unknown, unknowable. It envelopes us in isolation, pushing us to feel inconsequential and irrelevant; or perhaps masked—the real parts of our identity not worth uncovering. It speaks to our worth, our value, or lack thereof, leaving us feeling insignificant, unqualified, inadequate. It may even gnaw at that place deep in our bellies as it dares to suggest that if this is who I am, who will concern themselves about me? Am I even loved ... or worse yet ... lovable? Am I worth loving? What could I then possibly do for God? What purpose could He possibly have for me? Does *He* even love me?

These thoughts lead to that icy grip of abandonment and rejection taking hold of your soul. If this is how we see ourselves, we believe others must see us this same way. And then we question how God could see us in any other way than what we've already established deep in our hearts—even if it directly opposes what it says in His Word. When we carry this *less than* identity in our hearts, it overshadows our actions and behaviors, leaving our potential and talents, and even our character, undeveloped, unexpressed, and unrealized.

In this vacuum of inferiority, it is not possible to walk in the high calling of God. There is no question then, that the healing of our identity—understanding, knowing, and believing we are who God says we are, not the sum of our experiences, is critical if we are to live in the power and authority to which we are called as followers and imitators of Jesus Christ.

Pushing Up

> **Note:** I encourage you to take the time for the prayers and for all the Scripture readings and declarations; they are the invitation to Holy Spirit, from where the healing power comes.

A. Laying Down False Identity

We can only receive if our hands are held open. We need to be willing to let go of all we clasp on to so tightly—all the beliefs we hold about ourselves, others, and God, and how we believe God sees us. It is only from this place of surrender that God can begin to heal our identity, and show us who He created us to be.

The journey begins by laying down all the false beliefs in which you currently identify—your false identity, as noted by your own expressions of invisibility on page 20. If it does not line up with God's Word, it is false. (If you are not familiar with the Lord speaking to you in prophetic pictures, please see page 118.) Take a deep breath and step in. Finish the prayer with the present cry of your heart.

Prayer:

Dear Lord, I stand before you, exposed and vulnerable, ready to be real with You and with my own heart. Please help me to let my guard down; I am trusting You to be my protection. Right now I surrender the false identities of _____. I repent for believing and partnering with these lies rather than choosing to believe I am who You say I am in Your Word. Open my eyes and show me how You see me, know me, and have created me to be, so I can see myself in Your truth, not as the sum of my experiences in the broken world. Give me the strength to comprehend the love You have for me, which surpasses knowledge …

_____

_____

B. Surrendering Life Experiences

It is time to lay down all the circumstances that have led you to believe in your false identity, as shaped by your life experiences.

Use the left side of the following boxes to list the wounds that have negatively impacted your identity, as brought to your remembrance by Holy Spirit. Include the names of any people connected with the event. Put similar occurrences in the same box. Your list may contain specific incidents where you have felt such things as being uninvited, unloved, unworthy, not important, or rejection from individuals, etc. The purpose of this exercise is not to wallow, but to acknowledge the pain, be heard, and then surrender it to the Lord so your heart can let go of it. Include what you have believed about yourself because of the negative event. What did your heart tell you at the time? For example, "I am unloveable," "I don't matter."

Note: If you are unfamiliar in working with Holy Spirit in the context of seeking His revelation, try this: rather than attempting to generate or sort through memories on your own, just pray in the Spirit, or focus on a few words of prayer such as, "Show me please, Lord. Thank You, Jesus, thank You, thank You..." Then quiet your mind. Trust that what comes to remembrance is from Him, even if it doesn't seem to fit in right away, or it seems random. Some events will be obvious to you, but some you may have forgotten about, or you may not have believed they would have had such a strong impact on you. The more you engage with Holy Spirit in this capacity, the more clearly you will begin to hear Him, and the quicker revelation will come. And, as pieces fit together and healing becomes evident, faith that you are hearing from Him will deepen. You are His sheep. You do hear His voice.

Prayer: (Adapt as needed.)

Dear Heavenly Father, there have been so many times in my life where I have felt <u>invisible, unappreciated, abused, forgotten</u>. Lord, I do not want to be <u>invisible</u> any longer. Please help me take off the cloak of <u>invisibility</u> so I can be <u>seen</u> by You, by others. I want to have a voice so I can share what You have called me to share, and be who You have called me to be. Please bring to remembrance all the times in my life where I have been wounded in a way that has caused me to construct a false identity. I want to surrender them to You, and be healed.

In Jesus' name, I cast out any spirits of pride, rebellion, or fear that are trying to prevent me from humbling myself before You, hearing from You, and obeying Your voice. Keep my spirit soft and teachable. Baptize me in Your Holy Spirit, so I can walk through this in Your power. Wash me clean with the Blood of the Lamb. I pray this in Jesus' name. Amen.

Wounds from your life experiences
(What did you believe about yourself because of it?)

God's truth
(How God sees you.)

Reflect on each event, and forgive the person/s involved. Include God and yourself when needed. For those ones that are more difficult to forgive, speak the words out of obedience, and the Lord will honor it, eventually connecting the words out of your mouth with your heart. This may not be instant, but it will come.

Prayer:

Dear Lord, in laying this down at Your feet, I know I need to forgive those who have hurt me, so I can be healed. Please help me do this in Spirit and in truth. I cannot do this on my own. It is only through Your power that true forgiveness can come.

I forgive _____ for _____
_____
_____
_____
_____
_____
_____

On the right-hand side of the previous boxes, record God's truths about the situations as He reveals them to you. This revelation can come in such forms as Scripture, words, pictures, physical sensations, songs, or impressions put in your heart, or even through other people. It can occur immediately, or over a period of time, requiring you to return to this section. The Lord is always creative in how and when He chooses to reveal His truth to our hearts! You do not need to record something for each incident, as one revelation of truth is often the key to healing many similar wounds.

Prayer:

Dear Lord, thank You for Your truth in all of my experiences. Speak truth into my negative life experiences. Please show me how You see me in each situation. Put Your truth deep into my mind and write it on my heart. Unveil the lies I have been believing that have constructed my false identities. Open my eyes to see things the way You see them, so I can be who You created me to be.

Note: If you are struggling to hear revelation from God, seek a trusted partner to help you pray through the difficult area. As well, you may find that for a time after the exploration of a healing area, situations will continue to arise that encourage you to go deeper into your healing. Remember, healing proceeds in layers.

Prayerfully compare the truth God shows you about each event to what you have been believing about yourself. Break off each lie that has formed part of the foundation of your false identity and pray the truth of how God sees you—your true identity. If what you have believed about yourself differs from what God says, that is a lie. For example, if an event led you to believe people don't care about you, and God shows you many others care, and His Word says He cares, the lie would be, "No one cares about me." **Continue writing the prayer by asking God to put you on a firm foundation and rebuild the structure of your life into the way He originally intended it to be.**

Prayer:

Dear Lord, You amaze me with Your tender mercy and grace as You help me deal with this delicate area. I thank You. Right now, I come out of agreement with the lie that says

_____.

This is not the truth. Your truth says

_____.

I come out of agreement with the lie that says …

Bring the needed areas of repentance before the Lord for each experience you listed in the boxes, including doubt and unbelief that you are who He says you are, and knowingly or unknowingly partnering with these lies. Ask the Lord to heal your heart for each experience, as you surrender them into His hands.

Prayer:

Dear Lord, thank You for the revelation You have already brought to me. Please reveal to me any areas in which I need to repent for my response to an experience, agreeing with a lie, choosing to believe my experiences or other people rather than Your Word, or anything else that is not in alignment with Your truth. I ask You to heal my heart from all the wounds placed there from these experiences. I repent for … I surrender …

C. Grieving Things Lost

List the things you feel you have lost because of the lies you have believed. Surrender each one to the Lord, asking Him to heal your heart and help you walk through your grief. This can include such things as relationships, experiences, opportunities, joy, peace, having an impact and having a voice.

_____
_____
_____
_____
_____
_____
_____
_____
_____
_____
_____

D. Practicing Gratefulness

List some of the many blessings you have received from the Lord. Include such things as the times you have been acknowledged, chosen, and honored, and the people who have done so.

Prayer:

Dear Father, sometimes I can get caught up in focusing on the negative things in my life and overlooking the many blessings You have given me. There are many times in my life where I have been honored, blessed, and acknowledged. There are many people in my life who have helped me in so many ways. Help me remember these things when I fall victim to believing only the lies of the enemy. Every time I feel unchosen, please remind me of all these times in which I have been chosen.

_____

_____

_____

_____

_____

_____

_____

_____

_____

E. Listening to The Lord

Spend a few moments in quiet meditation and reflection before the Lord. Record any further words, pictures, knowledge, or understandings the Lord gives you as you wait upon Him. Record your ongoing revelations of *Who you are* and *Who God is* on pages 122-123.

Prayer:

Is there anything else, Lord? What do you say about all this? How do You see me? What do You wish to teach me, tell me, show me, reveal to me? Who did You create me to be? I open my heart to You. Please open my eyes and ears so I may hear more from You.

_____
_____
_____
_____
_____
_____
_____
_____
_____
_____

What Scripture reflects His truth about your identity?

_____
_____

His Truth

Speak the truth of Scripture out loud. Ask the Lord to write these truths on your heart.

So she called the name of the Lord who spoke to her, "You are a God of seeing," for she said, "Truly here I have seen him who looks after me."

Genesis 16:13

"Fear not, for I have redeemed you; I have called you by name, you are mine.

Isaiah 43:1b

I am the good shepherd. I know my own and my own know me, just as the Father knows me and I know the Father; and I lay down my life for the sheep.

John 10:14-15

And the Lord said to Moses, "This very thing that you have spoken I will do, for you have found favor in my sight, and I know you by name."

Exodus 33:17

"Before I formed you in the womb I knew you…

Jeremiah 1:5a

O Lord, you have searched me and known me! You know when I sit down and when I rise up; you discern my thoughts from afar. You search out my path and my lying down and are acquainted with all my ways.

Psalm 139:1-3

But even the hairs of your head are all numbered.

Matthew 10:30

Declaring His Truth

Speak these scriptural declarations out loud. Speak them often. Let your soul know He is the God who sees you.

My God is El Roi, the God Who sees me, the God Who looks after me.

My God sees me.

My God looks after me.

I fear not, as I have been redeemed.

He has called me by name. I am His.

The Lord is my good Shepherd.

He knows His own.

He has laid down His life for His sheep. He has laid down His life for me.

I have found favor in His sight. He knows me by name.

He knew me even before He formed me.

He searches me and knows me. He knows when I sit down and when I rise up.

He discerns my thoughts.

He knows my path and all my ways.

He knows every intimate detail about me … He knows me.

He sees me.

Thank You, Lord, for seeing me, knowing me.

Unit Two
My Princess Heart

Prophetic word - February 2017

God is taking you into a season of "Jocelyn." It will be a season of identity.

—Jeff Barnhardt

In the midst of a season of identity, pondering that very thing is a logical course of action. I was doing just that while driving to school one day. "I know how to fight. I am a warrior." My close friends know this about me. (Ask me about my dagger!)

"Don't forget about the *Princess* part ... You are My Princess Warrior."

My breath caught and tears threatened to expose how deeply the Lord's words penetrated my soul ... for that *Princess* part had been long lost. I needed to have the princess part of my heart restored. I needed to believe I was loved, treasured—even cherished.

> Journal entry - May 20, 2017
>
> Lord how do You/I heal my "Princess" heart after it has been so battered and bruised ... after I have felt so untreasured, uncherished, unimportant? How do I/You begin to make me feel worth pursuing? I know this has been true in my life experiences, but it is not Your truth. Help me see myself as You see me. Help me be able to open up my heart to receive Your love fully, beyond measure, so it overflows with love. If I can't receive and overflow with Your love ... I can't love others like You have designed me to love. I need to be pressed down, shaken, and overflowing with Your love until it spills onto my lap and the lap of others.

> *How is my crown restored? I think this is part of letting people take advantage of me ... always having to rescue. I don't have to be valuable by doing everything for everyone, being everything to everyone. I can't do it. I can only do the things You call me to do.*
>
> *Lord, what are the wounds that have made me feel so not loved, not worth anyone's time? Please, Holy Spirit, I ask for revelation.*
>
> *I break off the lie that I am not worth pursuing. I repent for partnering with this lie and passing on this valuelessness to my kids by my actions and beliefs ...*

And so began the quest to put the crown, given to me on the day of my salvation by my Father, the King Himself, back on my head. It required the smashing of a stronghold: lie after lie, bound together, holding the core lies of my false identity securely in place. Rejection wound after wound came tumbling out from deeply buried parts of my heart. Names of people and circumstances, many long forgotten, revealed themselves in the pages of my journal. Some had played major roles in my life and caused big, gaping holes—still bleeding. Sometimes it was only my response and beliefs about them that caused this very hole. Perceived rejection still causes a wound if that is the lens though which we view things. Some remembrances were seemingly so insignificant I couldn't believe they would be among the things and people revealed—yet if something receives enough pinpricks, it weakens and is easily torn. So it was with my heart.

As lie by lie unraveled, one layer exposed revealing another false belief underneath, I finally reached one of the core lies on which I had built my life; on which I had set up circumstances and allowed or disallowed people in my life, and the vows I had made to keep that part of my false identity so securely in place.

It was maddening because it was a lie hidden in plain sight—one of the most devious of hiding places. It was sort of a phenomenon in my life. I had known about it, talked about it, wondered about it—but had never understood its full impact, had never dug beneath it, nor had I asked God for His revelation about it. Finally bringing it to the Lord, I asked the question. *"Why did I never like any of the men who liked me ... no matter how amazing they were? And why, especially, why did I suddenly stop liking the ones I was interested in, as soon as they started liking me?"* Time and time again, I would run away from all those to whom I had been so strongly attracted—as soon as they turned their affections to me. Why was it that my feelings mysteriously disappeared the moment this attraction was discovered to be mutual? It made no sense—until the undetected lie that ruled my behavior patterns was revealed.

Though it seemed deceptively harmless, the lie at the root of this issue ended up sabotaging parts of my life and robbing me of the potential for healthy male relationships. *"The boy I like is never going to like me."* This is what I had told myself—the lie that was placed in my young teen heart, as one of my first relationships quickly disbanded with his unfaithfulness. It became my vow, the vow I unknowingly persevered hard to keep in place through much of my life. And it grew, as all infections do, into, "People I like are never going to like me," and finally manifested as, "The man I love will never love me." Once I understood this lie was at the core of my false belief system, I could see the patterns of how it had operated in my life. If the boy I liked never liked me, the reverse had to then be true. The boy who liked me ... I could not like him. Subconsciously, this vow governed my beliefs and forced my feelings to correspond. These lies also became an open invitation—allowing unhealthy people, ones who could never love me, to rule over my life.

Finally, after all these years, I came out of covenant with these lies, and barred them from continuing to be a part of my identity. I was now ready and free to allow God to heal and restore that princess heart of mine.

Journal entry - May 20, 2017

I am Your creation and You desire me healthy, whole & happy. You have good things for Your daughter. I AM ROYALTY. I AM YOUR DAUGHTER. THIS MAKES ME A PRINCESS. I CAN FIGHT. THIS MAKES ME A WARRIOR. I AM YOUR PRINCESS WARRIOR. I AM CHOSEN BY THE ALMIGHTY KING, CREATOR OF THE UNIVERSE. I WILL WALK IN YOUR PURPOSES, IN THE FULLNESS OF MY SALVATION AND DESTINY.

Pushing Up

A. Practicing Gratefulness

A grateful heart is good soil for healing.

Write a few heart-felt words to express your appreciation to one or two of those people in your life who have accepted and loved you, and have made you feel important.

Prayer:

Lord, there are people in my life who have provided a measure of healing; those who have been Your hands and feet, showing love to me. I thank You for them.

_____

_____

_____

_____

_____

_____

_____

_____

_____

_____

B. Dismantling Walls

The expressions of rejection wounds can be extensive:

- abandonment (connection)
- abuse (love)
- anger (calmness)
- insecurity (security)
- co-dependency (security)
- depression (joy)
- disappointment (hope)
- envy (goodwill)
- fear (courage)
- frustration (support)
- self-harm (safety)
- stubbornness (surrender)
- unforgiveness (forgiveness)
- grief (joy)
- hate (love)
- hopelessness (hope)
- trauma (health)
- isolation (community)
- jealousy (generosity)
- sadness (joy)
- pride (humility)
- rebellion (unity)
- performance orientation (acceptance)
- shame (honor)
- anxiety (peace)

Highlight any of the expressions of rejection you feel have manifested in your life. Add to the list if necessary. Pray to release them.

Prayer:
O Lord, Heavenly Father, I come before You, heart in my hand, and giving it to You. I trust You with these so very vulnerable pieces of me. I lay down my _____ (expression of rejection from the above list) God, it is Yours to carry. Please take it. Fill me instead with Your _____ (the opposite of your expression of rejection). (Repeat as needed.)

C. Revealing Targets

Ask the Lord to reveal the key times in your life when the crown has been knocked off of your head.

Prayer:

Now Lord, I am ready to go deeper. I am willing to "go there!" I want to know all the ugly memories stored in my heart, put there by rejection, which are holding me back from truly understanding myself as Your accepted and loved child of royalty. I ask You, Holy Spirit, to reveal the wounds I have received which have made me feel not so loved, not worth anyone's time, or _____.

    Lord, as I explore these deep wounds of rejection, whether they were inflicted upon me intentionally, through neglect, indifference, or unintended oversight, please go with me. Help me be courageous and willing to confront all the things You show me. Bring to remembrance the key issues I need to face so I can walk through the pain, on the road to my complete healing. I ask for revelation as to what vows I made or lies I have believed that have formed part of my false identity. Show me who I am as You see me.

Rejection Wounds:

_____

_____

_____

_____

_____

_____

What did you tell your injured heart because of these events? What lies did you believe? (Lies may seem true in your life experiences, but they are contrary to Scripture and what God has for you.) **Did you make any vows because of believing the lie?** (Vows sound like: "I will never … I will always …" For example, "I will never trust anyone again!" is an inner vow.) Remember to follow the strategies for Holy Spirit revelation rather than trying to think them up on your own.

_____
_____
_____
_____
_____
_____

Ask the Lord to open your heart to receive from Him all He has promised you. Ask Him to show you how He sees you in this context. What is the truth He is whispering to your heart?

_____
_____
_____
_____
_____
_____

D. Removing Targets

Declaration:

Lord, I break the lie that _____.

I declare Your truth, the one that says _____.

I cancel the vow _____.

The truth is _____.

I repent for believing this lie/making this vow. I will not partner with it any longer. I come out of all covenants with it, and I align myself with Your truth of who I am. I take this target off my back, right now, in Jesus' name. Please heal and seal my wounds.

(Repeat for each lie and vow from page 41.)

E. Walking in Forgiveness

God asks us to forgive those who have rejected us. Are you ready to let go of your hurt so you can grasp on to your healing?

Prayer:

Lord, there are also people in my life who have taken me for granted, abused me, hurt me, rejected me, and left me feeling unworthy and insignificant. But I know that as long as I hang on to it, only resentment can grow. I do not want that to be a part of my heart. Please help me to do this. Right now, I choose to forgive them. I choose to forgive _____ for _____. I choose to forgive _____ for _____.

F. Perceived Rejection

Sometimes what we have believed and received as situations of rejection are, in reality, only the result of a faulty perception, viewed through the lens of an already wounded soul. We may have unjustly held another accountable for holding the sword of these woundings. It is time to lay down all blame so the chains that bind us may be broken and unity may be restored.

Prayer:

Dear Lord, it is time to lay down all of my offenses and woundings at Your feet. Take them, Lord, all of them. I now know I may have been holding offense against another, believing they were at fault—yet I am the one who is acting as the unjust accuser. Please forgive me. Please heal and seal all those wounds, because they are still very real to me and just as painful. Please show me if there is anyone I need to make peace with in my heart. Teach me the truth of the situation so healing and freedom may come to all of us.

The Lord showed me:

_____
_____
_____
_____
_____
_____
_____
_____

G. Walking in Repentance

Are there people in your life who you have taken for granted or rejected?

Walk through healing in this area by bringing it before the Lord in confession.

Prayer:

Lord, there are also people in my life who I have taken for granted, hurt, and rejected. Please forgive me. Help me to see others as You see them, and walk in the same love for others that Jesus does. If there is anything You wish me to do for restitution, please reveal it to me and give me the courage and opportunity to carry it through.

The Lord showed me:

_____
_____
_____
_____
_____
_____
_____
_____
_____
_____

H. Listening to the Lord

Take some time while your heart is still open and exposed to commune with the Lord. Let Him pour His oil into all the gaps and raw places, and whisper His revelations into your soul. Write/draw your discoveries to preserve this time with Him.

His Truth

Speak the truth of Scripture over yourself. Let these verses sink deeply into your heart. Highlight the one that resonates within your spirit the most.

See what kind of love the Father has given to us, that we should be called children of God; and so we are.

1 John 3:1a

The Spirit himself bears witness with our spirit that we are children of God, and if children, then heirs—heirs of God and fellow heirs with Christ…

Romans 8:16-17a

For we are God's masterpiece.

Ephesians 2:10a (NLT)

But you are a chosen race, a royal priesthood, a holy nation, a people for his own possession, that you may proclaim the excellencies of him who called you out of darkness into his marvelous light.

1 Peter 2:9

You are the light of the world. A city set on a hill cannot be hidden.

Matthew 5:14

No, in all these things we are more than conquerors through him who loved us. For I am sure that neither death nor life, nor angels nor rulers, nor things present nor things to come, nor powers, nor height nor depth, nor anything else in all creation, will be able to separate us from the love of God in Christ Jesus our Lord.

Romans 8:37-39

Declaring His Truth

Declare the truth of who you are in Christ—your true identity. Add your own revelations as they are opened to you.

> I am a child of God, loved by the Father.
>
> I am an heir of God, and a fellow heir with Christ.
>
> I am God's masterpiece.
>
> I am a chosen race, a royal priesthood, a holy nation, and God's own possession.
>
> I am the light of the world. I will not be hidden!
>
> I am more than a conqueror.
>
> I cannot be separated from the love of God!

_____
_____
_____
_____
_____
_____
_____

Unit Three
Stand Up, Girl!

> You are not going to have the inner strength and power to stand up for yourself until you believe you are worth standing up for. [Others] treatment of me did not determine who I was. I know who I am.
> —Kimm Reid

My methods of handling conflict throughout my life have been reminiscent of a mini volcano. I would let unrelated issues pile up until I hit the point of exasperation, then unload, unconcerned about where, when, or with whom. Though my explosions were not, by any means, full force rages of anger, swearing, and violence, they definitely led me to harshly say inappropriate things in obnoxious and self-righteous ways, without much sensitivity or respect to the feelings of others.

The Lord showed me that though I may have been right in my view of the situation, I was wrong in how I handled it, or didn't handle it, making me the unrighteous one. There are many times in life when you need to stand up for others, but you also need to stand up for yourself and for what you believe. I couldn't do this on a regular basis; didn't until I felt pushed right back against that proverbial wall and then lashed out as it became an issue of self-preservation. This systematic conflict avoidance put me in a position of tolerating things that should have been intolerable; I passively accepted treatment of me that I should never have allowed to happen. I was unwilling to walk away, until the situation was dire.

As God started healing my identity in this area, His question was, *"What would happen if you stood up for yourself?"* I prayerfully examined this question, and my responses became more revelatory as I walked through each one of them, eventually unraveling more and more lies at the core of who I believed myself to be, or perhaps, not to be.

"Standing up for myself, sticking with who I am, puts me in conflict where there would be a potential of hurting, disappointing, and offending others. They would then be mad at me, or won't like me. If they don't like me, they won't bother with me, will walk away—abandoning me."

"What does that tell you about yourself—make you believe about yourself?" the Lord asked.

"… That I'm not worth pursuing. I'm not worth the effort. I have not enough value for people to invest in me!" was my breaking-heart's cry.

I had developed a mentality that caused me to have to do everything it takes to avoid conflict and please others, even if it meant not voicing my opinion, not standing up for myself—becoming silenced … invisible. I had become responsible for others in ways that were unhealthy, including trying to control their feelings. I could not, *would not* allow them to be hurt or disappointed; especially not disappointed in me—no matter what it cost. This response proved disastrous. I would overextend myself to take care of the needs of others, often neglecting things in my own life to do so. I ignored their bad behavior, and even concealed their secrets if that was what was expected. I did everything in my power to *make* people want to be with me, be connected to me, and see it as worthwhile to be in relationship with me—even if that meant I had to give up who I truly was, and what I believed in. I had succumbed to the enemy lie that I did not have enough value for people to want to invest in me.

A person in my life at one time told me I was like a dog at people's heels—tongue out, paws extended, begging for them to let me help. Though hard to admit, as hurtful as that ill-intentioned comment was, there was some truth to it. Though I absolutely believe in serving others to the best of our ability as God calls us to do, there has to be a proper balance so it does not become all-consuming, nor co-dependent, leading to the detriment or even the demise of ourselves or our families. It cannot become part of our identity. It is what we *do*, not who we *are*.

We have to see ourselves as having enough God-given value to not compromise who we are to become what they want us to be; even if it means saying, "No." We are not responsible for other people's feelings. We must allow them to walk their own journeys; it is, in fact, detrimental to their own growth and development to do otherwise.

I had become a people pleaser and an overachiever, instead of solely a God-pleaser. I had allowed myself to become a victim, and to numb my internal red flags that warned me I was not being treated as I ought to have been. I allowed confusion and invisibility to reign in my life, taking on an "I don't care" attitude, until I did … but by then it was regretfully too late, and I was past the point of tolerance—unleashing words which no one deserves, against both those coming against me and bystanders, alike.

Repentance done, restitution made, and wells of blessing and joy poured out through my prayers on all I have hurt with my words, I then asked the Lord to show me how He sees me. Being led to play the song *Priceless* by For King and Country, He quietly whispered that I was *"sought after,"* and *"worthy."* I was *"courageous, the most beautiful, and faithful."* He showed me a picture of a warrior, head raised in confidence, eyes closed in reverence, surrounded by a soft, golden glow. It was someone who could fight savagely for others if need be, but also for herself. She was worth it. It was a gentle, honoring picture—life-changing—and one that I'll always treasure as I learn to treasure myself.

Prophetic word - May 2017

You have been trained into being like … you don't belong here, don't stand up tall. You have been whipped into this place of less than … no, you don't qualify here. God says, "No! From this day forward, STAND UP, GIRL, STAND UP, GIRL! NOW IS THE TIME TO STAND UP, GIRL." He's lifting you up. Even if you want to droop over, you can't. Even if you want to be unseen, you can't, because He is putting you in the spotlight and it is good. It may be uncomfortable, but it is good. He's just lifting you up.
—Maryann Ward

Pushing Up

A. Shedding the Mentality

Why do we allow ourselves to be inappropriately pushed around? Why is dealing with conflict so difficult for some of us? Why do we tolerate treatment that borders on abuse, or is flagrantly abusive? Why do we even then sometimes turn this very same hateful behavior onto others? Part of the identity we construct as we partner with lies of the enemy speak to the false belief that we are not worth standing up for—others may be, but we are not.

This mentality is set strongly in place, fortified by the construction of what The Genesis Process[1] refers to as *protective personalities*. As long as they are prevalent in our thought patterns, they will control our reactions and behaviors. To be free to confidently respond to conflict appropriately, we need to be free of all inhibiting protective personalities. They are not in line with who God says we are, and therefore are not a part of our God-given identity.

Read through the list of common protective personalities. Highlight the ones with which you identify. Add to the list if necessary. Then release them, following the sample prayer. You may have to return to this section periodically throughout your healing journey as further protective personalities are revealed.

(From The Genesis Process. Used with permission.)

- Doormat
- Blank
- The Phony
- Invisible
- I'm ok
- Nice
- Numb
- The Perfectionist
- The Wall
- Over Achiever
- The Pleaser
- The Martyr
- The Victim
- Confusion
- The Rescuer

Prayer:

Holy Spirit, please show me the traps of the enemy that I have fallen into, believing that they were a part of my personality; believing they have kept me safe.

I release _____ (names of protective personalities) from my life. I will not partner with them any longer. I don't want them. I don't need them. They are not a part of my God-given identity. I ask you, Lord Jesus, instead, to guard me from any wounding in this area I have been guarding against. Thank You for protecting me.

B. Stop Pushing

As hard as it is to face and admit, we can also be on the other side; we can, at times, be the ones pushing others around. These are still self-protective behaviors: a *"get them before they get you"* mentality. They are not in line with our true identity.

Highlight any of the following protective personalities in which you have operated, either currently, or in the past. Add to the list if necessary. Then, release them, following the sample prayer.

- ✦ Anger
- ✦ The Protector
- ✦ Control
- ✦ Don't mess with me
- ✦ The Critic
- ✦ Independence
- ✦ The Intimidator
- ✦ The Bully
- ✦ Needy (Passive Aggressive)

Prayer:

Lord God, I repent of operating in these behaviors. I do not want them to be a part of my life. I will no longer identify with them. I release _____ (names of protective personalities) from my life. I will not partner with them any longer. I ask you, Lord Jesus to keep me from wounding anyone with these behaviors. They are not a part of me. Thank You, Lord, for protecting me and keeping me safe, so I don't have to feel always on the offensive.

C. Releasing Control

Controlling others is not godly behavior—even if in doing so you are only attempting to keep them from being hurt. You are not responsible for other people (outside of parental/guardian responsibilities to some degree), nor for their feelings. It is time to relinquish this control, giving it over to the Lord.

Ask Holy Spirit to reveal any circumstances in which you need to let go of all control. Then pray to release it.

_____

_____

_____

_____

_____

_____

_____

_____

Prayer:

Dear Lord, You who control the sun and the moon are much more capable to orchestrate things in my life than I am, and You are certainly more able to take care of the people in my life than I am. I am ready to now give You ultimate control over my life. I also give up my attempts to control others in all capacities, even in those areas where I have mistakenly believed it was beneficial. Lord, I give you control in the specific areas of … (list areas revealed above.)

D. Coming Out of Alignment

What lies and vows have been revealed as you read and worked through the selected material? **Ask Holy Spirit to reveal any lies you have believed or inner vows you have made that have falsely become a part of or have clouded your identity. Break them off and speak the Spirit-revealed truth into your life as you work through the following prayer:**

Prayer:

Dear Lord, thank You that I only have to speak Your truth, and the lies of the enemy are shattered! In Jesus' name, I break off these lies that have tricked me into believing in an identity that is not me. (Break off the lies that have already been revealed. Then listen quietly for Holy Spirit to bring any new revelation into your mind.)

I come out of agreement with the lie that says _____

_____

_____

This is not the truth. Your truth says _____

_____

_____

I cancel and come out of alignment with the vow_____

_____

_____

The truth is _____

_____

_____

What Scripture reflects the truth about who you are?

_____

_____

_____

E. Seeds I Have Planted

When we fail to handle conflict in a godly manner, there are always negative consequences. Our reactions, behaviors, actions, and words, intentionally or not, can end up hurting others; those around us and those we hold most dear. We can end up contributing to their pain and discouragement, rather than being the light and the hands and feet of His love that Christ asks us to be. Galatians 6:7 says, "Don't be misled—you cannot mock the justice of God. You will always harvest what you plant" (NLT).

The choice of our responses can also ultimately hurt us—our credibility weakened, relationships damaged or destroyed, our own healing delayed. We need to offer restitution for this in the ways we can. **Let's pray.**

Prayer:
Dear Heavenly Father, I have made some unwise choices in my life; ones that have led to negative thoughts, words, and actions that have caused wounds in myself and in others. Please forgive me. From this day forward, through Your mercy and grace, help me to replace my negative thoughts, words, and actions with those of blessing and encouragement.

I pray that every negative seed I have planted or that was planted in myself and others in each situation of conflict I have faced throughout my life be ripped out, roots and all, right now, in Jesus' name. I pray every future effect of that bad seed be immediately stopped, in the name of Jesus. I pray, Lord, that You plant Your seeds of truth, faith, justice, love, peace, healing, and salvation in their place.

I pray that every person I have ever hurt with my behaviors and words, including myself, be filled to overflowing with the oil of joy, so abundantly that it spills over into all we say and do, and overflows into the lives of all those around us, impacting them with Your glory, for Your glory. Thank You for forgiving me. I forgive me, too. Please reveal to me if there are any people I need to forgive, or from whom I need to ask for forgiveness.

As well, Holy Spirit, please show me if there are any actions I need to take, or words I need to speak to put right any of the specific situations in this area. I ask for Your wisdom, and the strength and courage to be able to carry out Your wishes for restitution. Thank You for Your healing grace. Amen.

Listen to the Lord and record any thoughts, words, images, or things you sense you need to do to make restitution with another.

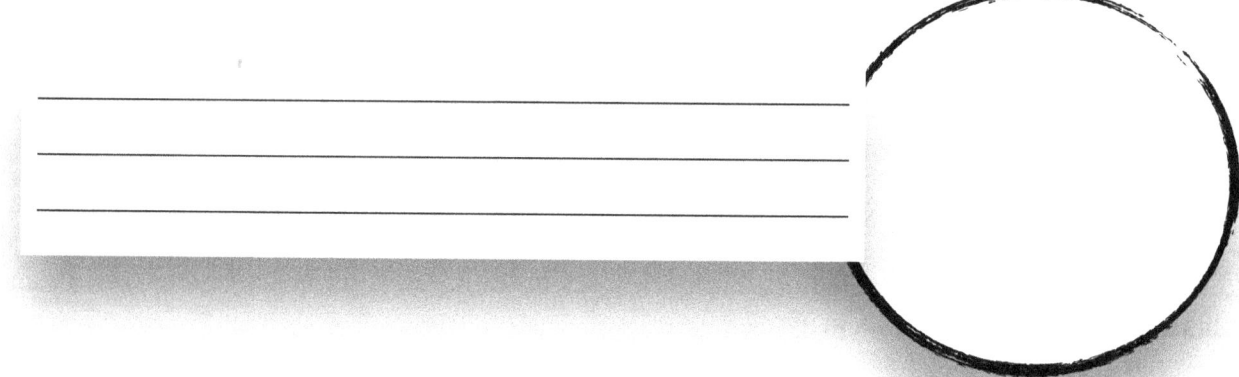

F. Conflict as Sabotage

Every time conflict, or the potential for it arises, ask the Lord what the enemy is trying to prevent by driving a wedge between the people involved. Instead of readily stepping into the conflict, ask Him what His purposes are for the relationship, and do what it takes to step into that, rather than falling into the trap of sabotage set by the enemy.

Examine several situations where a conflict or the potential for it had arisen, but was resolved in a godly manner. What were some of the positive outcomes from that relationship? What was the enemy trying to block?

Do you have an unresolved issue/conflict with someone? What might the enemy be trying to sabotage? Is there anything you need to do about it?

G. Grieving Things Lost

List the things you feel you have lost because of the lies you have believed, vows you have made, or the mistreatment you have endured. As you surrender each one to the Lord, ask Him to heal your heart and to help you walk through your grief.

H. Listening to The Lord

Rest before the Lord for a few moments, listening to His still, small voice. Record any of the words, pictures, understandings, knowledge, truths, or assignments the Lord gives to you. Be sure to quickly follow through with any actions He asks you to take.

His Truth

Speak these Scriptures out loud over your life. Let them teach you to stand strong!

For the eyes of the LORD run to and fro throughout the whole earth, to give strong support to those whose heart is blameless toward him.

2 Chronicles 16:9a

For freedom Christ has set us free; stand firm therefore, and do not submit again to a yoke of slavery.

Galatians 5:1

…but just as we have been approved by God to be entrusted with the gospel, so we speak, not to please man, but to please God who tests our hearts.

1 Thessalonians 2:4

For am I now seeking the approval of man, or of God? Or am I trying to please man? If I were still trying to please man, I would not be a servant of Christ.

Galatians 1:10

Pay attention to yourselves! If your brother sins, rebuke him, and if he repents, forgive him…

Luke 17:3

Because you are precious in my eyes, and honored, and I love you …

Isaiah 43:4a

Like a muddied spring or a polluted fountain

is a righteous man who gives way before the wicked.

Proverbs 25:26

The LORD looks down from heaven on the children of man, to see if there are any who understand, who seek after God.

Psalm 14:2

"For thus says the Lord GOD: Behold, I, I myself will search for my sheep and will seek them out. As a shepherd seeks out his flock when he is among his sheep that have been scattered, so will I seek out my sheep, and I will rescue them from all places where they have been scattered on a day of clouds and thick darkness.

Ezekiel 34:11-12

Praying His Word

Pray through His Word to you that you may be strengthened.

My God, You are the God who seeks me; and in Christ, You have set me free!

Keep my heart blameless before You, O Lord, that Your arm may give me strong support!

Help me to stand firm and not submit again to a yoke of slavery; that is not Your plan for my life.

Help me to speak not to please man, nor to seek his approval, but to please You, LORD, and You alone.

LORD, I pray that You may test my heart and find it worthy; help me to be a true servant of Christ.

Help me to be mindful of my thoughts and my actions, honoring myself as You would have me honored, as I am precious in Your eyes, and You love me dearly.

Help me to forgive those who trespass against me and help me not to give way to the wicked, falling into their schemes and traps. Help me to be righteous—like pure, fresh spring water; a sparkling fountain flowing with the river of life.

Thank You for looking down on me from above, watching me, teaching me, rewarding me, as I seek diligently after You.

Thank You for seeking after me, the sheep of Your flock, rescuing me when I am scattered in my dark days of the storm.

I pray this in the precious name of Jesus. Amen.

Unit Four
Steps of My Own

"No, I could never do that!" Being the strong introvert that I was, this is what my mind screamed when I received that first phone call asking me to present a session at an upcoming educational conference. But somewhere deep inside, I knew it was what I truly wanted to do. It was almost, in fact, as if I was born to do it.

My session was a success, and it opened the doors to presenting at many more workshops and conferences at provincial and national levels for over ten years. Being invited to sit on provincial committees, and receiving a high level of recognition in the province, school and division, followed. Being well known in my niche of education also opened the door to writing resource material for two separate publishing houses, and establishing a company of my own.

I eventually would attend many sessions where the facilitators would be sharing my materials, and I would often receive recognition in some form by the facilitator or participants.

Soon, however, with having my children, and then having to sort out what had become a messy life, the door closed on that chapter of my career.

Several years later, as I tried to re-enter the teaching force and this time as a single parent, I couldn't even secure a position within the new division to which I had moved. This was a huge rejection to me. Pride rose up and pushed me to be indignant: *After all I have contributed to the education system...* Anger followed suit: *I have freely mentored several principals in this division and many of their teachers, and now they won't even hire me!*

I eventually did receive employment through a string of interesting events. But, with everything I had to deal with as a newly single parent with small children, and needing time to pursue my own emotional healing, I chose to step into the shadows rather than attempt to resurrect any of my previous professional accomplishments or involvements. By the time I was ready to continue in the vein of my former endeavors, much time had passed and I was virtually unknown and unrecognized ... invisible. It appeared that the door to all such opportunity had been firmly closed.

Over the next few years, jealousy began to squirm its way out of my being as I watched others progressively receive the types of recognition and opportunity that had once presented themselves to me, while my slate seemingly remained blank. I couldn't, or perhaps *wouldn't* understand why everyone around me was receiving opportunities, while I, being just as qualified and capable, I judged, was not. I questioned as to why others were chosen and I was overlooked. Was I not "good enough?"

But God, ever more concerned about our character than our advancement, grabbed this opportunity as a "teachable moment." Thus, for the next several years, He began the process of rooting out of me the pride, arrogance, jealousy, and anger that had portrayed themselves in my temperament. I was given ample opportunity for confession, public repentance, and apologies for the words I had spoken, and for my actions, or lack thereof.

Through this discipline of the Lord, I began to grow in my trust and faith. He challenged me to believe that He has put me on a specific path that will take me to where He wants me to go, as long as I am faithful in following His leading. I had to learn to trust that He would bring me every opportunity I needed for the advancement of my unique journey. I had to realize that I can't take the steps He has prepared for others, as they will not take me to where I need to be—I would actually be pushed off my own path. It had nothing to do with being "chosen" or "not chosen," being "good enough" or "not good enough." These experiences were simply *not* part of the steps in *my* journey. They would, instead, be only a distraction, keeping me from where I was supposed to be, and doing what I was supposed to be doing.

It was pride rearing up that had said, *I knew how it should go* better than the Lord God Almighty, Creator of Heaven and Earth, who knows all that is and shall be. And it was anger and jealousy that kept me from hearing His voice as He tried to lead and guide me. Any envy or coveting on my part over the path of others, He revealed, will only end up holding me back from achieving the Christ-like character I need to walk forward along the path God the Father has specifically designed for me. I can still hunger for more, but always for *the more* of what He has designated for *me*, not for others; every thing that will bring me closer to walking in the fulness and abundance He has for *my* life, and into *my* calling.

I had to absolutely eradicate from my mindset the concept of comparing myself to others, whether it be spiritually, professionally, emotionally, or physically. There are still times where confusion sneaks in as an opportunity I believed was on my path is given to another. It is at these times, however, that the Lord asks me to lay my crown at His feet and surrender, in trust, that He is still in control, He still has plans for me, and they are still good (Jeremiah 29:11).

As I look back over my life and reflect on my experiences, I can see how intricately everything in my life has fit together to prepare me for the very path on which the Lord now has me. I can finally see how elaborately my life was crafted to teach me and train me, lead me and guide me, so I am able to complete every task to which He has called me. Everything I have been through—the good, the bad, and even the ugly—have all worked together so I can walk in the destiny the Lord had planned for me before the beginning of the ages.

Pushing Up

A. Looking at Your Heart

When you honestly take inventory of your heart, do you compare yourself with others? What is the result?

Highlight any words which stand out as you prayerfully consider them. Write out any specific instances or situations the Lord reveals to you. Bring these before the Lord in prayer.

- ✣ pride
- ✣ anger
- ✣ judgment
- ✣ doubt
- ✣ confusion
- ✣ jealousy
- ✣ envy
- ✣ arrogance
- ✣ rebellion
- ✣ _____

_____
_____
_____
_____
_____
_____
_____

Prayer:

Lord God, I come before You, heart in my hand, honored that You love me and know me so well as to create a unique path just for me. Thank You for leading and guiding me in Your wisdom, so I may fulfill all the good plans You have for my life.

Lord, I repent for comparing myself to others, for not honoring the unique path You have given me, and for thinking I might know better the way I should go than You, the One who created the heavens and everything in it; the One who knows the beginning from the end. Right now I bind up and cast off the spirit of _____. I come out of alignment with it. I will no longer partner with it in any manner. (Repeat as necessary with the words from the previous list.) In their place, Lord, release the fruit of the Spirit: love, joy, peace, patience, kindness, goodness, faithfulness, gentleness, and self-control.

Bring each of the specific situations before the Lord, asking for forgiveness for any negative thoughts or actions on your part. Ask the Lord to help you forgive any of those you feel you need to forgive. Ask Him to reveal the truth to you about each of those situations: what is He teaching you through them? What part of your character is He revealing? How might it actually be preventing you from walking in His full plan of abundance for your life? **Record His revelations as He speaks them to your heart.**

Ask the Lord if there are any actions of restitution you need to take in regard to anyone harmed through any of your words or actions as you walked in the pain of comparing yourself to others.

_____
_____

B. Opening Doors

Are there any doors you have been opening, trying to open, or frustrated that they have not opened, that may not be directives from the Lord?

Ask Him for revelation about these doors, and then bring it to God in prayer.

Prayer:

Dear Lord, I thank You that You have plans to prosper me and to give me a hope. I am sorry for trying to open doors on my own, without seeking Your guidance and waiting for Your timing. I close those doors now, realizing that they may be a distraction from Your design for my life, and are only pushing me off that path You have created for me. Specifically, I close the doors of:

_____
_____
_____

I ask You now, Lord, to open the doors of opportunity in all areas of my life that You have designated for me, in Your perfect timing. I hunger and thirst after You and all You have for me. Increase my trust and faith in You and Your direction for my life. Help me to hear Your voice ever more clearly as I seek You with my whole heart. If there are things that need to be sanctified in me before I can walk through any of the doors You have for me, please bring that to my attention, and show me what I must do. I ask You to help me walk in complete obedience. I pray this in the precious name of Jesus, my Lord. Amen.

C. Surrendering Your Will and Your Agenda

Are there areas in your life where stubbornness has set in, and you find yourself *wanting what you want, when you want it,* either in your bigger ambitions—your *will*, and/or in your daily walk—your *agenda*? *If you struggle with the "No one is going to tell me what to do!" protective personality, return to page 51 to release it.*

Ask the Lord for His thoughts in this area. Maybe it is time to surrender your crown and ask Him to be seated on the throne of your life.

Prayer/Revelation:

D. Listening to the Lord

Come before the Lord to settle your heart and seal the healing work. Ask the Lord if there is any further work needed to be done in this area, such as losses to grieve, or lies in which you need to come out of agreement with. Ask the Lord to give you a Scripture that will speak to your soul in this area.

Scripture:

His Truth

Speak the truth of Scripture out loud over your life, and come under its guidance.

For You *are* my rock and my fortress;

Therefore, for Your name's sake,

Lead me and guide me.

Psalm 31:3 (NKJV)

Furthermore, because we are united with Christ, we have received an inheritance from God, for he chose us in advance, and he makes everything work out according to his plan.

Ephesians 1:11 (NLT)

Blessed be the God and Father of our Lord Jesus Christ, who has blessed us in Christ with every spiritual blessing in the heavenly places, even as he chose us in him before the foundation of the world, that we should be holy and blameless before him.

Ephesians 1:3-4

A man's steps are from the LORD; how then can man understand his way?

Proverbs 20:24

Oh, how great are God's riches and wisdom and knowledge! How impossible it is for us to understand his decisions and his ways!

For who can know the LORD's thoughts? Who knows enough to give him advice?

Romans 11:33-34 (NLT)

Trust in the LORD with all your heart, and lean not on your own understanding;

In all your ways acknowledge Him, and He shall direct your paths.

Proverbs 3:5-6 (NKJV)

Show me Your ways, O LORD; Teach me Your paths. Lead me in

Your truth and teach me,

For You *are* the God of my salvation; On You I wait all the day.

Psalm 25:4-5 (NKJV)

If you need wisdom, ask our generous God, and he will give it to you. He will not rebuke you for asking. But when you ask him, be sure that your faith is in God alone. Do not waver, for a person with divided loyalty is as unsettled as a wave of the sea that is blown and tossed by the wind.

James 1:5-6 (NLT)

And He was withdrawn from them about a stone's throw, and He knelt down and prayed, saying, "Father, if it is Your will, take this cup away from Me; nevertheless not My will, but Yours, be done."

Luke 22:41-42 (NKJV)

Declaring His Truth

Make these scriptural declarations out loud.

The LORD is my rock. He is my fortress.

I have received an inheritance from Him!

He chose me in advance, before the foundation of the world!

He has blessed me; in His eyes I am holy and blameless.

He works everything out according to His plan; He gives me my steps.

His ways are unfathomable; how then, can I understand?

How can I give Him advice?

The riches and wisdom and knowledge of the LORD are awesome.

In Him, I can trust with all my heart.

He shall direct my path, show me His ways, and teach me His paths.

He will lead me in His truth as I wait on Him all the day.

I will not waver! I will not be divided. My faith is in God alone.

Not my will, but His, be done!

Unit Five
Linking Shields

Prophetic word - August 2014

I see the Lord reminding you that He has surrounded you with a shield of strength. You have many godly relationships in your life and the Lord just encourages you to stay in that place, even though you are being healed and good things are coming. But He says, "Jocelyn, know that I am protecting you. I am a shield, but I use people to be the shield."

He has surrounded you with relationships that are a strength for you. And He says, "Jocelyn, there is nothing wrong with that."

I feel that at times there is an accusation of the enemy that says, "How come you are not strong enough? How come you have to turn to this person or that person? Why do you have to stay in that place?"

And the Lord says, "No, no, I provided that. I am your shield. I am your rear guard and I use people to do that, and I will keep you surrounded, Jocelyn. I will keep you surrounded even after the days when there is more freedom ..."

—Val Byrd

For one of them, the Lord just pointed her out amidst the congregation and said, "That one!" And so it was. We became fast friends of the heart. For others, feeling a strong connection in prayer, I felt I was just not to let them go. Feelings mutual, our soul-to-soul prayer times continued. Some friendships grew slowly as I healed and changed, blossoming into a mutual love and respect for each other. Others were quick—from acquaintance to feeling like we had been friends forever in sheer moments, pouring love, wisdom, and understanding into each other. And still other people came along to pick up the many pieces of me when I needed it the most; shelters in the times of my storms.

Though we are all a part of God's larger community of believers with whom we are to walk in unity and in love, there are those in our closer community that form our tighter, inner circle—the ones we allow access to our heart; the ones who have the most impact and influence on our lives. And God has richly blessed me over the years with these ones—the amazing ones who have my back, with whom I link shields; together with whom I will fulfill my destiny.

This is why community is so important, and why God puts us in community. But sometimes we forget that part—the part that it is *God* who puts us in community. Instead, we sometimes stubbornly chase those people and relationships we consider "more desirable," and we potentially miss the ones with whom God is actually placing us in a relationship of deeper intimacy.

After much heartache and too many wasted hours, I eventually learned this. Some of the best relationships I now have are not the ones I would have chosen on my own, or had they not heard from the Lord, they would not have chosen it. I wonder how many godly relationships I have overlooked throughout the years as I too, kept focused on those I tried to choose, rather than allowing God to put me in community.

How many times have I chosen to feel hurt and offended over chasing relationships that God did not ordain; that were not meant to reach the degree of intimacy I desired? Though at times I felt rejected and wounded by these people, this was most often not their intention. It was simply a case of God not putting me in their inner community; and at times, God protecting me from that very thing. Close relationships require intense investments of time and heart. And realistically, there is only so much time and heart one can afford to give, thus limiting the number of close relationships that can be maintained. It is therefore not feasible that every one of our friendships or those of our acquaintances will reach that friends-of-the-heart level.

And we need to graciously extend this same freedom to others—even if it means we are not allowed inner-most access in their lives—without perceiving it and receiving it as personal rejection, and casting our offense on them. We cannot allow ourselves to fall into the enemy trap of believing the lie that they did not choose us because we are not "desirable" or "worthy enough" to be their close friend. Rather, as we lean in hard in pursuit of the Lord and listen closely to His voice, He will put us in community with like-minded, like-hearted people—the Caleb to your Joshua, the Elisha to your Elijah.

He will align you, often in supernatural ways, with the people whose destinies are interconnected with yours, bringing you together in His perfect timing; perhaps for a season, perhaps for a life-time—and at times for but a moment. Some relationships become like a puzzle picture fitting together. When you have your specific pieces in place, and they have their pieces in place, He fits you together, each one being able to provide pieces for the other, filling in the previously missing holes and gaps. Had you met too soon, without all the necessary pieces in place, the meshing that needed to occur would not have been possible.

However, there are those times in our lives when we *don't* have all our pieces together; we don't even know where many of them are! It is then that the Lord forges another type of relationship—those that help reconstruct the lives and hearts of the ones in need. One person, in partnership with the Lord, pours into the other in different ways, holding them up until they can stand on their own. Though they should not expect anything they give to be reciprocated, the Lord teaches, blesses, and fills them through the relationship, making it mutually beneficial, and in the end, often gives them more than they gave. Having been on both sides of this type of relationship, I *know* this to be true. And it becomes even more of a blessing and honor when, having been held up by another, the Lord allows you to pour back into their lives, as you rise up and become strong.

There is also a place for investing in others, sacrificing for them, being an integral part of their lives, perhaps even releasing destiny over them—while they do not even know that you were the Lord's chosen vessel to do so. As the Lord calls you into His secret place to war in the heavens for them, He may ask you to remain silent—never acknowledged by man, never seeking their approval. It is enough that your Father in Heaven knows your heart, sees your obedience, sees you. It is then that it is not about you, your accomplishments, your recognition, your glory. It is then that the glory truly is given to the Lord in Spirit and in truth. And it is then that the Lord trusts you, and opens more the door of opportunity, with more detailed and intricate assignments, creating your new path, taking you to higher levels, and deeper into Him.

There are perhaps as many types of relationships as there are people. God has put many different people in my life in various seasons to fulfill specific purposes in my life. Some I laugh with; others I cry with—many I do both. As long as I put God at the center of each relationship, asking for an understanding of what He wants to bring out of it—out of me through it—instead of forcing my own purposes, He will continue to put His godly people into my life, in His time. The Lord has used and will use them to add to my strength, my shield, my wisdom, my peace, and my joy. They go before me. They come behind me. I am surrounded.

Pushing Up

A. Taking Account

As you think back over your life, ask the Lord to bring to remembrance all those who currently or have at one time or another formed a part of the circle of people surrounding you; people who have chosen you, stood with you, poured into you, and perhaps picked up the pieces of you.

Write your name in the inner circle. Record their names in the bigger circle.

Thank You, Lord, for every person You have so carefully designed to be a part of my life!

B. Confronting the Pain

Challenges cannot be overcome if they are not acknowledged. Take an account of the situations where relationships did not unfold as you had hoped. This is not about blaming people or putting them in a negative light, but if a relationship, or lack thereof, is evoking an unhealthy emotional reaction, you cannot move forward until there has been healing. Once the wound is healed and sealed, you are free to move into the inner community God has ordained for you. Adapt the prayer as needed.

Prayer:

Dear Lord, thank You for giving an ear to hear the cries of my heart. There are times in my life in which I feel all alone. I feel overlooked by the people around me, unnoticed, and unimportant. Yet my heart craves to be seen, acknowledged, loved. I long to be important in their eyes. This is what hurts, Lord:

Note: You may find that you have to work through this unit several times as new layers are exposed.

_____
_____
_____
_____
_____
_____
_____
_____

C. Exposing the Lie

Ask the Lord to expose the lies you are believing. Remember, it may feel like the truth of your circumstances, but it is not God's truth.

Prayer: (contd.)

I don't understand why they seem to have chosen others, and not me. This hurts my heart, and it damages the way I see myself. When I think of the rejection in these situations, I believe

_____
_____
_____

(Ask Holy Spirit to reveal the lies you are believing. Do any vows need cancelling?)

But God, I know that is not Your truth, so I break off those lies. I refuse to believe them or partner with it. I choose instead, to believe Your truth. *I am accepted. I am Jesus' friend. I am chosen of God. I am* _____

Please help this truth start being apparent in my life. This is the truth in which I choose to walk.

D. Healing and Releasing Hearts

Are you ready to ask the Lord for healing, and to release others to be healed?

Prayer:

Lord, anywhere I have been hurt in my pursuit of relationships that were not necessarily of Your design, knowingly or unknowingly, I ask for healing in my heart. I also release each of these people to You. I release … (individually release each person/situation from Part B.) Help me know in my heart that my lack of relationship with them does not speak **in any way** to my self worth, only to the different directions of our paths. I hold no offense against them, but release them from any and all expectations I have put on them.

(Continue to release them each time another incident occurs. It often takes perseverance to stand in God's truth. Do not expect to have an absolute absence of feelings when these situations occur—you are human! The intensity of those feelings, though, will not be as severe, and their duration will decrease each time you release them.)

E. Finding Your Tribe

The Lord wants to surround you with your people! Ask Him to start/continue this process.

Prayer:
Lord, I know Your truth says I have no lack, for You supply all my needs according to Your riches in glory by Christ Jesus. And one of my needs is community. I need to find my tribe of like-minded, like-hearted people; ones who can stand with me, laugh with me, cry with me, and help me grow closer to You. Help me to be content with every role You have given me to play in each life You bring across my path, big or small, acknowledged or confined to that secret place of prayer. And help me to be content with the roles others have been ordained to play in my life. Help me see relationships as You see them. Help me see myself and others as You see us.

Please bring me those people I am to invest in—those ones who it is more so about them, rather than me. Bring me those ones as well, who are to pour into me, and those with whom I am to link shields, standing together as a tribe in Your army, bent on sharpening one another. I surrender myself to Your choice of those with whom You will surround me, and to Your will in every aspect of those interactions. I repent for any of the times I have forced my purposes on relationships. (Ask the Lord if you need to repent for anything specific.)

Draw me to the ones You want me to pursue, and help me to continually release those I have been drawn to only in the flesh. Keep my motives for relationships pure and holy. Help develop the godly character in me and in those around me during our times together.

Holy Spirit, right now I ask You to show me if there is anyone You have put on my path that I have overlooked or neglected. (Take a moment to listen. If He shows you someone, continue with the prayer.) Lord, I repent for not listening to Your voice and being obedient in

Your purposes for me. Lord, I bring _____ (the person He showed you) before You, and I ask You to cultivate our relationship into whatsoever You desire. Help me see them as You see them. Help me stand tall by their side and walk with them as long and as far as You call me to do so. I pray this in Jesus' name.

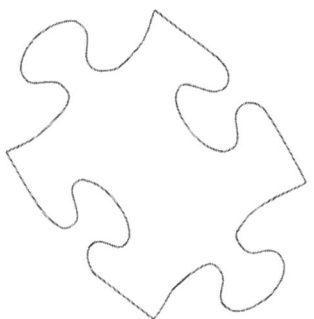 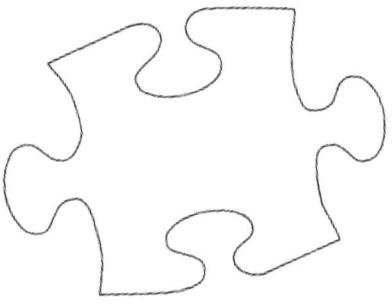

F. Missing Pieces

Though it can be hard, we need to be open to the correction of the Lord. Woundings to our hearts can cause us to be missing pieces of ourselves. In this brokenness, we can operate in ways that are detrimental to relationships. This can include behaviors that are:

controlling, disloyal, mean-spirited, harsh, impatient, bitter, jealous, angry, hard-hearted, demanding, excessively submissive, patronizing, critical, judgmental, crude, abusive, sharp, unkind, ungracious, offensive, sarcastic, austere, disconnected, rude, chaotic, unyielding, ...

With an open and vulnerable heart, come before Him and ask if, in your woundedness, you have acted toward anyone in a manner that was not pleasing to the Lord. Highlight any of the words from the previous list that tugged on your spirit, and then confess them before the Lord, repenting and renouncing (turning from) the behavior. Ask Holy Spirit for help in changing the behavior. Ask Him to then fill you with love, loyalty, kindness, patience, soft-heartedness, goodness, and self-control. Ask Him to restore any of your missing pieces so you can join those destined to walk with you.

G. Filling in the Spaces

Ask the Lord to show you His heart toward you. Pray that His thoughts of you sink deep into every part of you where negative roots were removed. Record this experience in such ways as words, Scriptures, prayers, and pictures.

His Truth

Speak the holy Scriptures aloud. Ask for wisdom and understanding as you read them, so you can learn their truths.

Therefore if *there* is any consolation in Christ, if any comfort of love, if any fellowship of the Spirit, if any affection and mercy, fulfill my joy by being like-minded, having the same love, *being* of one accord, of one mind. *Let* nothing *be done* through selfish ambition or conceit, but in lowliness of mind let each esteem others better than himself. Let each of you look out not only for his own interests, but also for the interests of others.
Philippians 2:1-4 (NKJV)

Live in harmony with each other. Don't be too proud to enjoy the company of ordinary people. And don't think you know it all!
Romans 12:16 (NLT)

As iron sharpens iron, so a friend sharpens a friend.
Proverbs 27:17 (NLT)

Listen to advice and accept instruction, that you may gain wisdom in the future.
Proverbs 19:20

And Elijah said to Elisha, "Please stay here, for the LORD has sent me as far as Bethel." But Elisha said, "As the LORD lives, and as you yourself live, I will not leave you." So they went down to Bethel.
2 Kings 2:2

> Two *are* better than one,
>
> Because they have good reward for their labor.
>
> For if they fall, one will lift up his companion.
>
> But woe to him *who* is alone when he falls,
>
> For *he has* no one to help him up.
>
> Again, if two lie down together, they will keep warm;
>
> But how can one be warm *alone*?
>
> Though one may be overpowered by another, two can withstand him.
>
> And a threefold cord is not quickly broken.
>
> **Ecclesiastes 4:9-12 (NKJV)**

Let us think of ways to motivate one another to acts of love and good works. And let us not neglect our meeting together, as some people do, but encourage one another, especially now that the day of his return is drawing near.

Hebrews 10:24-25 (NLT)

"Again I say to you that if two of you agree on earth concerning anything that they ask, it will be done for them by My Father in heaven. For where two or three are gathered together in My name, I am there in the midst of them."

Matthew 18:19-20 (NKJV)

Praying His Word

Pray through His Word to receive His wisdom and understanding.

Oh Lord, God Almighty, thank You for wanting to surround me with like-minded people of Your community; the ones with whom I will fulfill my destiny. Keep me in one accord, of one mind, and in harmony with Your people. Keep me from operating in selfish ambition, but let me esteem others better than myself, truly caring about them and their lives. I stand against all pride that threatens to prevent me from enjoying the company of those You put in my path.

Sharpen me through each relationship You graciously put in my life. Help me to humbly receive their godly advice and instruction, so that I may gain wisdom.

Bring me into those God-ordained Elijah-Elisha relationships, so we can walk this journey together, true travel companions, helping each other up when we fall, and keeping us from being overpowered. I ask for those two, together with whom I can be part of a threefold cord that is not easily broken, that we can motivate one another to acts of love and good works, continually encouraging one another, and gathering together to agree in prayer.

Thank You for the people You have put and are putting in my life, adding to my strength, my shield, my wisdom, my peace, and my joy. Thank You for those that go before me. Thank You for those that come behind me. Thank You for surrounding me.

In Jesus' name, I pray. Amen.

Unit Six
Letting Go

Why, Lord, why would You put them in my life, so close to my heart, only to rip them away again and again? As I look back over my life, I see a sad trail of people ... leaving. Some joined another in marriage and began walking another path, some were called to another part of the country or even continent. Some slowly drifted off, our focuses changing, unraveling the bonds that once tied us together. Others were severed more harshly; offense driving a deep wedge.

I have suffered so many losses, Lord ... it would have been easier if they were never even in my life ... With that confession, the Lord showed me what would have been my life—big, gaping holes where each one of those had once walked, needed skills left untaught, characteristics still unforged. Breaking off that lie, I asked the Lord, "How then, do I lessen the pain of continually saying good-bye to those I love, and after a broken or lost relationship that may never be restored?"

"You see them as I see them. You see the purposes for which I put them in your life. They help Me lead you where you need to go. But the path of each journey—yours, theirs, is different, and may only intersect for but a moment. With a grateful heart, you see all the good, the growth, and the wisdom that came because of it, and you hold them loosely. You understand that I will always have people walk with you in your journey, but they will not always be the same ones. They will come and go, teaching you, stretching you, encouraging you, lifting you, carrying you, challenging you, stirring you, prodding you, provoking you—whatever you need at the time. You love them, care for them, cry with them, run with them, then let them go, knowing I will always be the One giving you what you need, choosing the hands that pour into you, and the feet that walk alongside you."

With that key understanding tucked snuggly into my heart by the Lord, I was finally able to rest in the release of my lost relationships. I could let go of my sadness for those gently taken out of my life by circumstances. And, perhaps more importantly, I could release my bitterness and anger over the relationships that ended less than amicably, and trust in God and in His higher purposes for them. I have learned that sometimes people are in your life for a specific season or purpose—they have what you need at that place in time, but once you are no longer in that space of mind and heart, your journeys perhaps may go separate ways. We cannot demand more from them than their allotted purposes, or more than they are able to give—or should give … and vice versa. It is in doing this very thing that we set ourselves up for rejection and unhealthy relationships that do not contain the necessary boundaries.

Injuries to our heart and lies put in our mind by the enemy over the years can result in a deep fear of being alone, which wreaks havoc on our perception of these proper relational boundaries. It can drive us to demand more out of people than is healthy or godly, or it can allow us to tolerate those very demands on us, which can be equally, if not more so, devastating. I have, regretfully, walked on both sides of that coin. Though God can turn the effects of all relationships to the good, using them to teach us and mold us into who He needs us to be, this fear of being alone can draw us, in our disobedience, into relationships He never intended us to have. And it can prevent us from walking away when our wise counsel, and every part of our rational selves screams for us to do so. We fall prey to such lies as, "I'd rather be in an imperfect/unhealthy relationship than in no relationship at all."

This puts us in a precarious position, choosing another person (who most likely is operating out of their own woundedness as well), above God, and leading us down a path we would not have chosen, had we truly known its eventual reality. Rather than seeking God for confirmation about being in the relationship, or hearing His voice about walking away, we tune Him out and let our fears, confusion, loneliness, and emotions lead the way, choosing instead to compromise, justify, and rationalize, and making a worse choice with each step deeper into it. And in these destructive relationships, as our identity is chipped away with the excessive demands, we become less than who we are, who we were meant to be. By the time we are ready to walk away—know our survival depends on walking away—there is sometimes not enough left of us to be able to do so …

Pushing Up

A. Lost Ones

As you take a survey over the years of your life, record the names of family and friends who at one time or another played a significant role in your life, but no longer are by your side. Their exits may have been graceful or not so graceful. Record their names alongside the path.

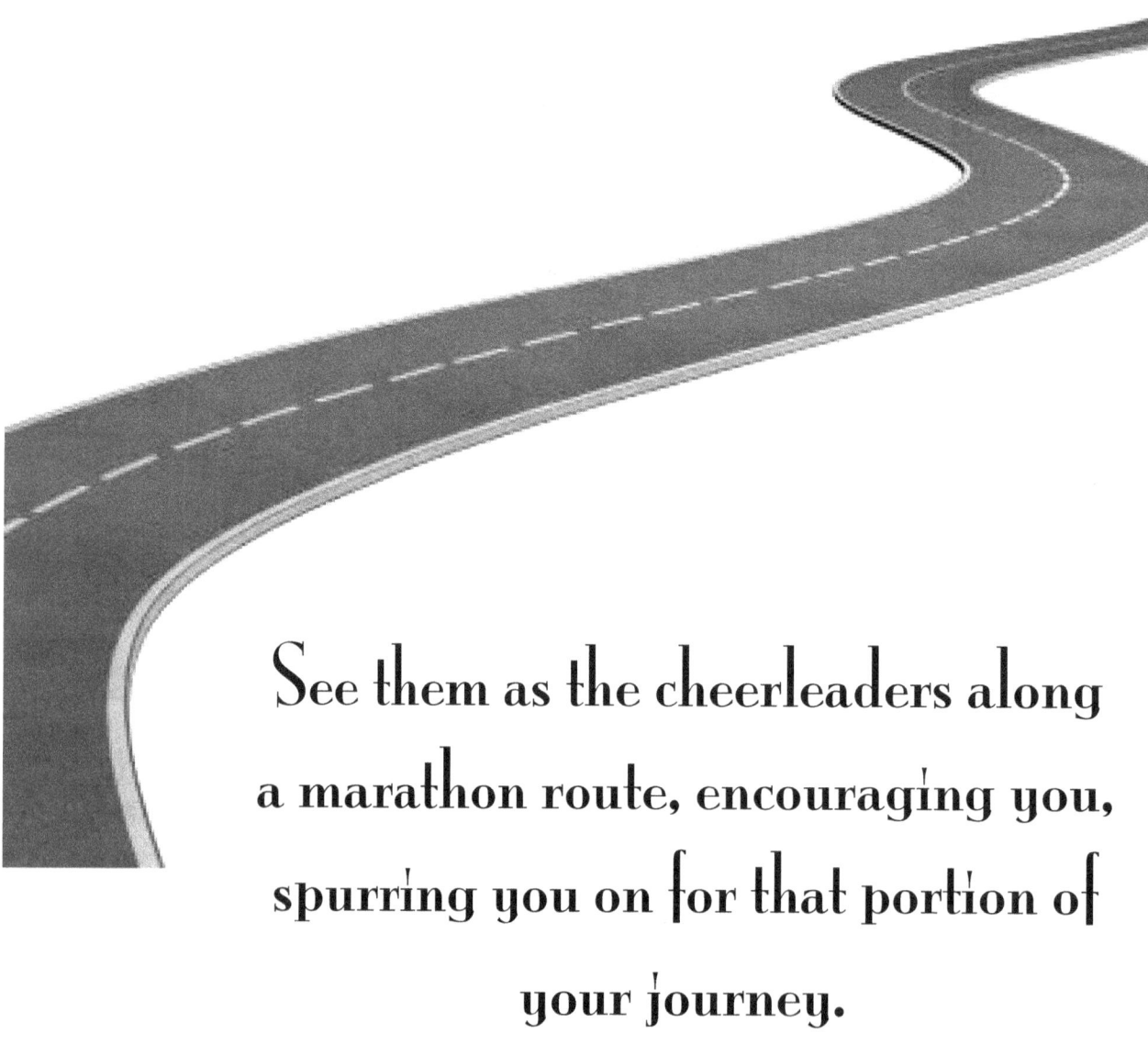

See them as the cheerleaders along a marathon route, encouraging you, spurring you on for that portion of your journey.

B. Examining Roles

Choose a few of the ones who played a more significant role in your life, or ones with whom you have never felt a sense of closure over their absence. Write their names and the roles they played in your life in the chart. Ask Holy Spirit to help you determine some of these main roles they filled in your life: things you learned through relationship with them, why you needed them at the time, how they may have filled in the gap, the good things that came out of it, the wisdom you received, how they may have stretched you, etc. Focus only on the aspects of growth and development, knowing great wisdom also comes through negative situations.

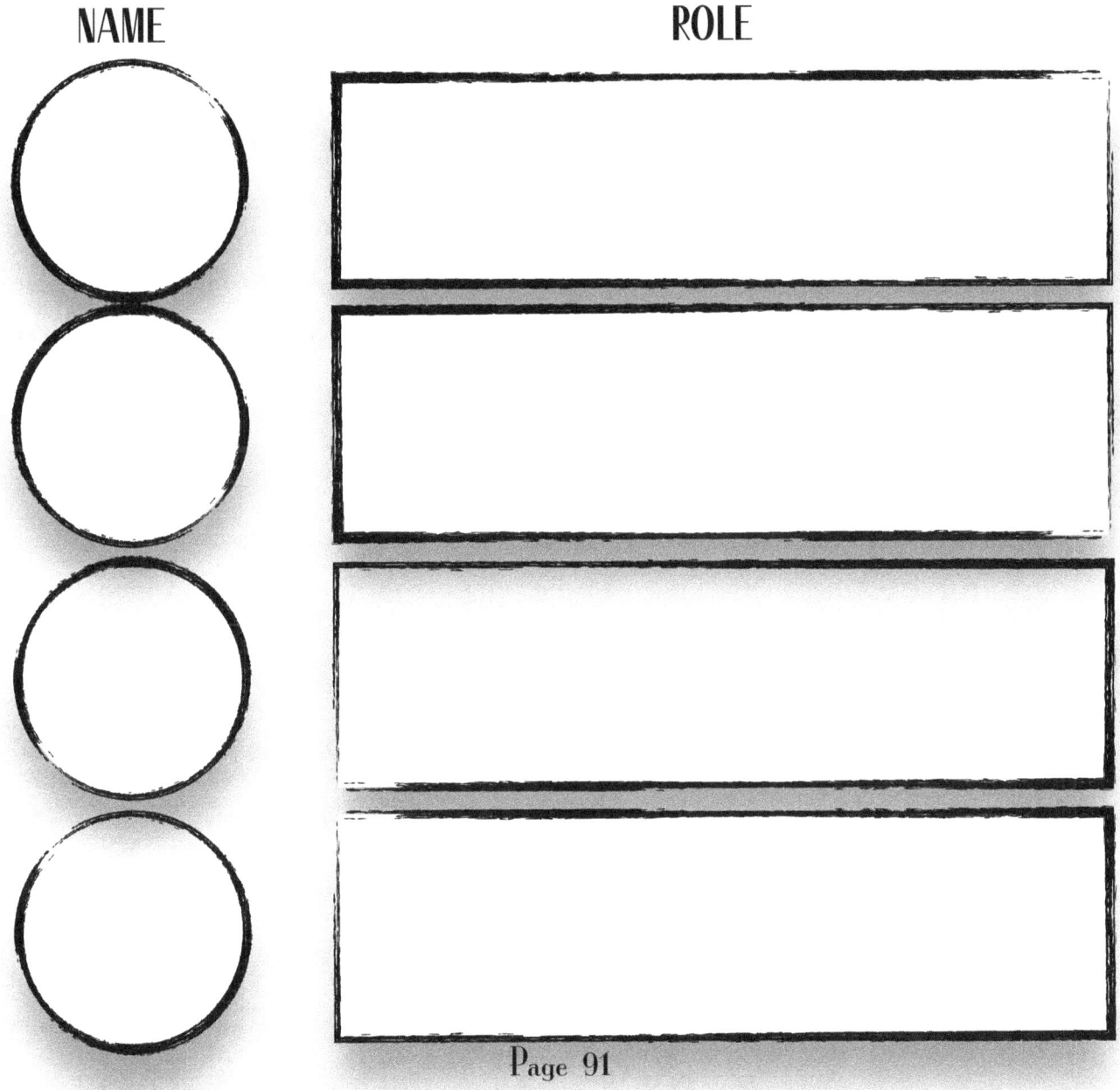

C. Being Grateful

Pray through the list of things you have received from these ones, thanking the Lord for each one as you read it out loud.

Ask Holy Spirit to show you what your life would have been like, what you would be like, had none of these ones been a part of your world. Record the revelations.

_____
_____
_____
_____

Thank the Lord for each one of the people in the chart and on the path. Write a prayer of thanksgiving to God for choosing to put them all in your life the way He did, in the time He did, for the time He did. Then pray a blessing over each one as you release them unto the Lord.

_____
_____
_____
_____
_____
_____
_____
_____

D. Letting Go

If you are struggling with a relationship that ended badly, work through the following section. If possible, have an honest conversation with the person to find out the information. If this is not feasible, trust the Lord's revelation. He wants peace brought to the situation as much as you do. It is amazing, perhaps even shocking, how very differently two people can see the same relationship as they look through the lenses of their own experience.

How do you/did you see the relationship?

_____
_____
_____
_____
_____
_____
_____

How do they/did they see it?

_____
_____
_____
_____
_____
_____
_____

Repent for your part in the loss of the relationship. If you are unsure of what your part is, ask Holy Spirit for revelation. **Ask for forgiveness from them if possible. Offer your forgiveness. Examine your heart.** Do you feel any bitterness, anger, resentment, jealousy, judgment, or other such negative emotions toward them or the situation? **Release them by surrendering these feelings to the Lord. Break off any offense. Ask the Lord to reveal to them any offense they are holding against you.** (Keep surrendering them as often as needed.)

Prayer:

_____
_____
_____
_____

Pray for healing and restoration of the relationship. It may not be restored to its formal state if it was not a healthy relationship with healthy boundaries. But as Christian brothers and sisters, we need to do whatever is necessary on our part to walk in unity.

Note the positive aspects of the relationship. What did you learn? What have you gained? What did you receive that you had needed at that time in your life? Remember, you must have needed something they could give you for God to have allowed it. Or vice versa. What were you able to give to them?

_____
_____
_____
_____

Thank the Lord for everything each of you gained throughout your time together. Accept the current relationship, even if it is not what you desire, by releasing it to God and putting them into His hands. Recognize that some people are not in a position/place to give you what you feel you need. Perhaps they have no boundaries, or are already overwhelmed. *Recognize this in yourself as well.* Relationships with no boundaries lead to co-dependancy. **Ask the Lord to help you make changes in your thoughts and actions to help restore the relationship, and/or to aid in future relationships. Ask the Lord for wisdom in understanding what an appropriate relationship should look like for each individual situation. Pray a blessing over the person.**

E. Walking Away

As Christians, we are to walk in love, unity, and forgiveness. While this is true, there will be times when the Lord asks you to walk away from a relationship for a time, or permanently, when it is damaging to you as His child, and to your relationship with Him. (Read Ezra 10). Though I have seen, and absolutely believe in the redemption of what may even seem like an impossible situation, there will be times when the Lord releases you from the relationship. But even when this is the case, making this decision can be exceedingly difficult. It is fraught with such feelings as failure, grief, fear, guilt, and inadequacy.

Prayerfully consider if the Lord is asking you to close the door on a relationship. This may include forgiving them and keeping them in prayer, but no longer having direct contact with them. *If you are in a situation where you are not safe, I highly recommend that you get out of the situation as quickly as possible, and continue seeking God from a safe place.*

Prayer:
Dear Lord, I come before You with a breaking heart. Help me to trust You more and more with this heart of mine, even when it hurts. I know You want the best for me, and sometimes the best for me may not be what I believe I want or think I need. You see the big picture, the whole, finalized tapestry. You know me and You know my life better than I do. Please reveal to me, Holy Spirit, deep in my heart, if there is someone I need to consider letting go of at this moment in my life. Speak to my heart, please, O Lord!

When you think of having to make this decision, what is your self-talk?

_____
_____
_____

What are the positive aspects of the relationship?

What are the negative aspects of the relationship?

How is this relationship impacting you as a person?

How is this relationship impacting your walk with God?

When you honestly examine the relationship over the length of it, is it becoming more healthy as you both work on it? Is the investment in change only one-sided? Is it spiraling downward?

_____
_____
_____
_____

Ask the Lord what He says about the relationship and its impact on you. Record His revelation.

_____
_____
_____
_____

If He is indicating you should close the door on the relationship for a time, or perhaps permanently, please pray with me.

Prayer:

Dear Lord, with Your hand You stretched out the heavens and laid the foundation of the earth. How much more so can You construct everything in my life in the way it should go; how much more so are You able to take care of me and my heart? Grow my trust in You and increase my understanding of just how deep Your love for me goes.

You want the best for me, for my life, for my family. You want me to walk in the fulness of everything for which You have created me. You want me in relationship with people that will help me to achieve this—to encourage me, build me up, love on me, and draw me closer to You. And You want me to do the same for the ones You place on my path.

Lord, You have shown me that <u>this one</u> in my life is holding me back, knowingly or unknowingly, from all You have for me, and preventing me from becoming who I was created to be. They are keeping my heart wounded and bleeding and they are keeping me from You. God, please give me the strength, courage, and fortitude I need to walk away, or even just take them out of my life in whatever way You ordain. Your will, Lord. I give You full permission and I trust You with this.

Please heal my heart, as there is always pain involved when two hearts, melded together, are ripped apart. I know the pain of loss will still feel great, even though this is for the longterm betterment of my soul. I cut off all soul ties between me and <u>this one</u> that are keeping us connected in the spiritual realm. Please fill the wound with Your healing oil and Your Spirit of love, joy, and peace.

Please keep me safe and protected when this happens. I break off every enemy assignment, tactic, or attack that may try to come against me that threatens harm to me or to my loved ones as this relationship is severed. Keep me resolute and steadfast in my desire to move forward with You and not look back or be drawn back into a damaging or unhealthy relationship with this person or with anyone else. Help me to cling to You and grow strong as You walk with me through these difficult steps of my journey. Grow my intimacy with You. Let me look first to You, then to others. Bring my healthy relationships into a deeper level of mutual love, respect, and intimacy.

I repent for my disobedience in the ungodly relationships I have allowed in my life. Please bring new people into my life to inspire and motivate me to become more like You. I want people in my life who have been where I want to go. I ask for those people to walk with me, mentor me, and help me grow, and to be a part of my life in all the ways in which You ordain them to be.

Lord, I thank You for Your love, Your mercy, Your grace, and Your patience with me as I learn and grow in the area of godly relationships. Keep me walking with You always.

My prayer is made in the mighty name of Jesus Christ. Amen.

His Truth

Read His Word to gain wisdom for difficult decisions in relationships.

He who walks with wise *men* will be wise,

But the companion of fools will be destroyed.

Proverbs 13:20 (NKJV)

There is one whose rash words are like sword thrusts,

but the tongue of the wise brings healing.

Proverbs 12:18

Faithful are the wounds of a friend;

profuse are the kisses of an enemy.

Proverbs 27:6

The righteous should choose his friends carefully,

For the way of the wicked leads them astray.

Proverbs 12:26 (NKJV)

Do not be deceived: "Bad company ruins good morals."

1 Corinthians 15:33

Do not be unequally yoked with unbelievers. For what partnership has righteousness with lawlessness? Or what fellowship has light with darkness?

2 Corinthians 6:14

Make no friendship with an angry man,

And with a furious man do not go,

Lest you learn his ways

And set a snare for your soul.

Proverbs 22:24-25 (NKJV)

And Ezra the priest stood up and said to them, "You have broken faith and married foreign women, and so increased the guilt of Israel. Now then make confession to the LORD, the God of your fathers and do his will. Separate yourselves from the peoples of the land and from the foreign wives."

Then all the assembly answered with a loud voice,

"It is so; we must do as you have said.

Ezra 10:10-12

Praying His Word

Pray through the Scriptures to open understanding in your heart.

Lord, thank You for the amazing people You have put in my life.

Help me to always walk with the wise so their words will continue to bring healing and restoration into my life; and help me to humbly receive their godly correction when it too, is needed.

Help me to always make my choice of friends and relationships honorable and pleasing to You, so I may always follow Your paths and Your ways.

Keep me from deception that my morals will forever be upright.

Keep me from being unequally yoked in all aspects of my life, but instead, in partnership with like-minded people who also walk in righteousness.

Help me to keep a wide path around those who walk in anger and fury, that they may not set a snare for my soul.

And Lord, please help me to continually separate myself from those that would draw me away from my precious relationship with You.

I pray this in the mighty name of the Lord of Hosts, Jesus Christ. Amen

Unit Seven
Held Accountable

> We acknowledge, O LORD, our wickedness
> *And* the iniquity of our fathers,
> For we have sinned against you.
> Jeremiah 14:20 (NKJV)

"Do you know anything about operating in the courts of Heaven? Robert Henderson[2] has done some excellent work in this field." This was the second time in just a few days the exact same information was relayed to me by two unconnected friends. The first time, I figuratively put the note she handed me on my *to-do* pile. With the second nudge, I realized God was saying it was not a *round-to-it* item, but rather, a *Right Now!* command.

I snapped to it with a condensed version of the information from a Sid Roth, *It's Supernatural* video.[3] I hesitantly applied the new knowledge several days later at a healing seminar—and watched in awe as the Lord broke heavy chains of generational bondage and freedom came—complete with a display of spiritual fireworks!

Several weeks later, a third friend, also from a different circle than the previous two, handed me a CD and a book about ... the courts of Heaven, by Robert Henderson; a fourth friend added the name Jeanette Strauss[4] to the mix. The importance of gaining a better understanding of how to operate in the courts of Heaven had become glaringly apparent. I strongly urge you to do your own research, but for the purpose of this guide, I will present my synopsis version, as I learned from the aforementioned resources.

There exists a courtroom in the spiritual realm, where satan stands before God, as in Job Chapter 1, and brings accusations against the people of the earth. He has built a legal case against us that threatens to disqualify us from fulfilling our destinies and receiving God's promises. If it is found that he has legal rights, he can remain in a position to tempt us and torment us in specific areas, and to interfere with God's plan for our lives.

These legal rights include unconfessed sin, unforgiveness, curses spoken over us or our bloodline, and generational sin. Patterns of behaviors and conditions that span across generations of a family line can indicate that a bloodline curse is in operation. Poverty, abuse, alcoholism, mental illness, premature death, anxiety, depression, and living in chaos are such examples. Strongholds, our own and that of our family, that have been fought against on the battlefield for years—but never broken—are also indications the enemy has legal rights to remain.

Though we do not bear the guilt of our forefathers if we have not walked in the same iniquity (Ezekiel 18), because that specific spiritual door has been opened, the accuser has been allowed, and will be allowed to attack us in the same areas over the entirety of our lifetime. This creates a likelihood of us stumbling in its wake at some point. Either way, it makes walking in righteousness in that area extremely difficult. In a dream, I once felt the forces of generational sin coming against a particular family I know. It was like getting hit head-on by a freight train—a force almost impossible to stand against. This is why closing the spiritual door through repentance is essential.

Battling these situations requires us to enter the courts of Heaven, approach God as Judge, and submit ourselves before the Father to see if there is anything in us—or in our bloodline—that is displeasing to Him. It is here, as we kneel before the throne, that we can ask for revelation as to what the enemy is using as a case against us—his legal rights—that are holding us, our family, in captivity.

As God the Judge reveals those accusations the enemy is holding against us, we are granted the gift of being able to repent on our own behalf, on behalf of our ancestors, and to stand in the gap and repent on behalf of our family until they can do so for themselves. This will close these spiritual doors. We can even repent on behalf of people groups, as did Daniel on behalf of Judah and Israel (Daniel 9:4-20). Repentance, releasing forgiveness, and the breaking of the generational curses nullifies the enemy's accusations against us. The case can be closed and we are released from captivity and from those unrelenting freight train-like spiritual forces coming against us. It is much easier to walk upright when we do not have gale force winds coming against us caused by these open spiritual doors. We can be free to receive the promises of God and walk full in our destiny.

As I witnessed firsthand the power for freedom from bondage in this realm of prayer, I sought to meet with my own family of origin in this capacity. We prayed to release those areas we recognized as patterns and behaviors in our generational line, and then those revealed to us as we presented ourselves before God our Judge. Upon confession and repentance, healing came to our family and we—including each of our kids—can now move forward into all God has for us without so many of the chains and snares from our collective past dragging us under.

Once my generational line was cleansed, the Lord began to once again refer me back to my own docket. I have been on both sides of the prayer line in the healing ministry for so many years—I didn't think there were still so many unexplored areas! But the Lord is ever faithful as He takes us through the sanctifying process to transform us more and more into the likeness of Christ. He brought to mind—repeatedly—that I had several *unfulfilled commitments.*

I didn't even know if that was technically sin, but the Lord readily assured me it was. I had made small monetary pledges to a charity and a political party over a year ago, but had yet to honor them. Their neglect was more due to inconvenience and carelessness than willful avoidance; they simply were not high on my priority list. However, after a few weeks of Holy Spirit's gentle insistence, I gritted my teeth in determination to complete the long overdue task—which took all of fifteen minutes.

Almost immediately, a friend handed me a book called *The Final Quest*, by Rick Joyner. This book is based on a prophetic dream he had, and in it was my confirmation:

"My Word is the power that upholds all things. To the degree that you believe My Word is true, you can do all things. Those who really believe that My Words are true will also be true to their own words. It is My nature to be true, and the creation trusts My Word because I am faithful to it.

"Those who are like Me are also true to their own words. Their word is sure, and their commitments are trustworthy. Their 'yes' means 'yes,' and their 'no' means 'no.' If your own words are not true, you will also begin to doubt My Words because deception is in your heart."[5]

Though my intentions had been honorable when I had made the pledge—I had not lied—it would become a question of integrity if I failed to fulfill it—which was likely to happen the longer it was neglected. Forgetting about things we've done—or failed to do—does not provide an adequate alibi in the courts of Heaven.

Our integrity can also be called to account if, in the misconception of being good stewards of the finances the Lord gives us, we take advantage of things that we do not have the right to claim. This can be as seemingly innocent as bending the rules on coupons or consumer deals and opportunities when we don't fully meet the criteria. This opens the door to deception entering into our hearts and amplifies that we are not trusting the Lord's provision—we have to find ways to do it for ourselves.

Luke 16:10-12 exemplifies how this can be detrimental in achieving our full potential in the Lord: "One who is faithful in a very little is also faithful in much, and one who is dishonest in a very little is also dishonest in much. If then you have not been faithful in the unrighteous wealth, who will entrust to you the true riches? (Read Isaiah 60!) And if you have not been faithful in that which is another's, who will give you that which is your own?" And yes, the Lord held me accountable in several discrepancies in this area.

But it didn't stop there. The next issue for which I was being held accountable was, to say the least, unexpected. Theft. This was a little shocking, as I am one who has held myself to high standards of integrity over the years. I was never a kid who stole candy from the grocery store; my mom never fed me grapes not yet paid for to keep me quiet while shopping. I had even paid for the lemon juice I had accidentally stolen as soon as I made the discovery. (The plastic lemon had rolled under my son's baby carrier, and I hadn't seen it while paying for the other items.) And yet … here it was …

As a teenager I worked at McDonald's, and I'd sometimes put Sprite in my crew cup instead of water. It was a common practice among the crew, and I hadn't thought too much about it at the time, or since. But now I was liable, and the account had to be paid. *How do I pay it?* I wondered. *I can't just walk into a McDonald's Restaurant and pay them. That would undoubtedly cause a problem when their register didn't balance, or they'd just pocket the money anyway,* I rationalized. *And besides, they'd think I was crazy when I tried to explain what I was paying for!*

How about a donation to Ronald McDonald House?

Fabulous idea, Holy Spirit! But how much? $20.00?

$100.00.

That's a lot of Sprite, Lord, at only pennies per glass ...

It was also a lot of money on the heels of my other recently-made paybacks and direct financial instructions of the Lord. Though my financial situation was not dire, I was already on a tight-rope walk of faith to keep food in my fridge and a roof over our heads.

Ouch, Lord.

But it had to hurt a bit. I found out later, it was symbolic—covering for all those other little things I had done along the same lines; other things I hadn't thought of as being theft, such as personal photocopies at work, since it was just one copy here, one there ... or the *I'll pay for it later* scenario ... but then I would forget. The payment encompassed all those things—things forgotten ... things unaware ... things the enemy was now using as legal rights in my life to continue to harass me.

How do I do this, Lord? Can I just send it in, or do I have to confess to someone? (I had already discussed this intriguing situation with a friend by this time.) *How about ... if they ask me, I'll tell them the story!? ...*

" ... and so, *why* did you decide to make a donation to Ronald McDonald House?"

I laughed, asked if she *really* wanted to know, and began to share my tale of restitution ...

Pushing Up

> **Note:** This unit represents healing in connection to family relationships, but also that of healing personal identity. Nothing is ever in isolation; everything overlaps. However, for the sake of keeping the content of the unit intact instead of spreading it out over two books, it shall all appear in Book 1.

A. Disconnecting the Dots

What patterns of negative behaviors and conditions have you observed that span across the generations of your family line?

_____
_____
_____
_____
_____

Bring each of those areas before the Father in repentance. Ask God the Father to forgive you, but also repent on behalf of all those who went before you in your family line—the iniquity of your fathers. Ask Holy Spirit to show you if there are any actions which need to be taken on your behalf, and on the behalf of your ancestors, to bring restitution to any situations.

_____
_____
_____
_____
_____

Stand in the gap for your family, repenting on their behalf until they are able to do so for themselves. This closes the spiritual door, making it that much easier for them to do so. (Consider yourself a forerunner!) Ask the Lord to bring your family members to a place of repentance in their own hearts. Ask Him to bring healing, restoration, comfort, and blessing to you and to your family members. Call upon Holy Spirit to show you how He sees you—your family, right now. **Record His revelation below.**

B. Entering the Courts of Heaven

Enter the courts of Heaven to determine what cases are being held against you and your family that may be delaying healing and walking in the fulness of Christ. After waiting on the Lord to hear His voice, record His revelation.

Prayer:

Dear Lord, I come before You as Judge and ask that You open the courts of Heaven that I may know the accusations held against me—that I may be held accountable for my own sin and the iniquity of my fathers. I fully submit myself to be judged by You. Help me to lay myself bare in my eyes, in Your eyes, that I may be purged of all sin and iniquity that lies within me. Make me brave. Make me strong.

I come on behalf of myself, my family, and my generational line, to the third and fourth generations. I ask for revelation as to what the enemy of my soul, my destiny, is using to build a case against us. Please reveal to me all his accusations that I may ask for Your mercy, Your pardon, as I lay myself in submission to You. I ask for You to show me, wherever possible, how I may make restitution on behalf of myself, and my family line. Lord, I seek Your heart—I seek to please You. I seek to do Your will. There is nothing else, Lord, but You. By Your Blood, I am set free. Thank You, Lord, for hearing my pleas, hearing my cries. I pray this in the name above all names, Jesus Christ.

Iniquities in my family line:

_____
_____
_____
_____
_____
_____

Ask Holy Spirit to show you specifically if you have any unfulfilled commitments, broken vows, or failures of integrity.

_____
_____
_____
_____
_____
_____
_____
_____
_____

Ask Him for a plan of restitution for these areas.

Follow the leading of Holy Spirit once you are given revelation. Ask for forgiveness, and begin to follow all the instructions He lays out for you. Record any areas where restitution is needed, and where forgiveness must be given or received. He may ask you to do a specific prophetic act to release something in the spiritual realm. You may sense you need to say or do something through the Lord, or in context with another person. It is imperative to follow through on all He shows you. Ask for confirmation in Scripture and through others if there are issues about which you are unsure or hesitant. Revelation may come immediately or over a period of time; or most likely—both. Revisit this process as often as necessary, until there has been resolution in each area of attack, and as new revelations are made. Finally, ask Holy Spirit to reveal to you how the Lord sees you and your family, right now, and in the future. Record anything further you need to remember about the unfolding of this process; both what was done and what you need to do.

C. Remembrance

Write a prayer of thankfulness to the Lord for His love, His grace, and His mercy. Choose a symbol which will remind you always of His nature of lovingkindness and draw it beside your words of gratefulness.

His Truth

Read God's Word and let what Jesus has done for us sink deep into your heart. He has made a way for us. His shed blood is the reason we can enter the throne room. Through His death on the cross and the resurrection, we have been redeemed and brought into righteousness with the Father. We can know peace and His Spirit will not depart from us.

Behold, the LORD's hand is not shortened, that it cannot save, or his ear dull, that it cannot hear; but your iniquities have made a separation between you and your God, and your sins have hidden his face from you so that he does not hear. For your hands are defiled with blood and your fingers with iniquity; your lips have spoken lies; your tongue mutters wickedness…
The way of peace they do not know, and there is no justice in their paths;
they have made their roads crooked; no one who treads on them knows peace.
Therefore justice is far from us, and righteousness does not overtake us;
we hope for light, and behold, darkness, and for brightness, but we walk in gloom. We grope for the wall like the blind; we grope like those who have no eyes; we stumble at noon as in the twilight, among those in full vigor we are like dead men. We all growl like bears; we moan and moan like doves; we hope for justice, but there is none; for salvation, but it is far from us.
For our transgressions are multiplied before you, and our sins testify against us;
for our transgressions are with us, and we know our iniquities:
transgressing, and denying the LORD, and turning back from following our God, speaking oppression and revolt, conceiving and uttering from the heart lying words.
Justice is turned back, and righteousness stands far away; for truth has stumbled in the public squares, and uprightness cannot enter. Truth is lacking, and he who departs from evil makes himself a prey. The LORD saw it, and it displeased him that there was no justice. He saw that there was no man, and wondered that there was no one to intercede; then his own arm brought

him salvation, and his righteousness upheld him. He put on righteousness as a breastplate, and a helmet of salvation on his head; he put on garments of vengeance for clothing, and wrapped himself in zeal as a cloak. According to their deeds, so will he repay, wrath to his adversaries, repayment to his enemies; to the coastlands he will render repayment.

So they shall fear the name of the LORD from the west, and his glory from the rising of the sun; for he will come like a rushing stream, which the wind of the LORD drives.

And a Redeemer will come to Zion, to those in Jacob who turn from transgression," declares the LORD. And as for me, this is my covenant with them," says the LORD: "My Spirit that is upon you, and my words that I have put in your mouth, shall not depart out of your mouth, or out of the mouth of your offspring, or out of the mouth of your children's offspring," says the LORD, "from this time forth and forevermore."

Isaiah 59:1-3, 8-21

Write your declaration on page 124.

Praying His Word

Pray God's Word in thanksgiving.

Thank You, Jesus, for making a way, through Your loving sacrifice of Your very life blood, to God the Father; that His strong arm saves me; that He does not hide His face from me; that His ears hear my cries. Thank You, God the Father, for washing the blood from my hands, from the hands of my family line. Thank You for bringing peace, righteousness, and justice to my path, through Your Son, Jesus.

Thank You for light and brightness overtaking me! Thank You for opening my eyes that I might see, and giving me life, full of vitality and power.

In overcoming the grave, Jesus, You have brought salvation, though my transgressions, sins, and iniquities have been great. My heart is full with Your sacrifice.

Keep me, Lord, from denying You, from turning my back on You in rebellion. Keep me from oppressing those around me, and keep my mouth speaking truth. Keep me walking in the way of Your justice, integrity, and uprightness. I want to live a life that is pleasing to You.

Thank You for sending Jesus as High Priest and Redeemer to intercede on my behalf and on behalf of my family. Help me to walk in righteousness, the fullness of my salvation, zeal, and passion to do Your will. Let me always walk in reverent awe of Your majesty, Lord, and to give all glory to Your name.

Thank You for Your covenant with Your children. Thank You that Your Spirit will not depart from my mouth, from my children's mouth, nor from the mouths of my children's children. I receive Your promise, Lord, this time forth and forevermore. Amen.

Appendix

Prophetic Pictures

Imagine laying on a white sand beach somewhere near the equator, with the hot sun gently warming every place of you. Picture in your mind, the brightly colored sails of the boats filling the horizon, gently rising and falling with the waves—the same waves that foam as they hit and break on the beach. Do you see it in your imagination? This picture that you can form on the movie screen of your mind is one of the ways the Lord can speak to us in pictures—only we don't conjure them up, they just appear. Often times they will change, going from one thing to another, and in this jump between the two pictures, a volume is spoken.

At one time I was frustrated with the Lord, inquiring as to why He couldn't just use words to explain things to me ... it would be so much more straightforward, specific, and direct. He uses words as well, but now that I have received pictures from the Lord for a period of time, I realize how much more can be said through pictures, in a fraction of the time. Even Jesus spoke in pictures as He shared the many parables with the crowds of His time. As you walk in it longer, practicing hearing from Him, you learn how to ask questions, explore, and speak it out. Often times, as I speak out what I see, that is when He will continue to fill in some of the gaps as to its meaning. This requires the belief and trust that He will be faithful in giving us more about the picture as we are willing to take the risk of speaking it out.

I am Found

What is your new self-talk? Highlight the words with which you identify, and all the ones which you wish to speak into your life. *This* is where your journey begins. I am…

- ☆ visible
- ☆ unmasked
- ☆ confident
- ☆ noticed
- ☆ seen
- ☆ unveiled
- ☆ known
- ☆ significant
- ☆ God's child
- ☆ fully developed
- ☆ enough
- ☆ irreplaceable
- ☆ chosen
- ☆ invited
- ☆ not forgotten
- ☆ consequential
- ☆ more than
- ☆ forgiving
- ☆ creative
- ☆ loving
- ☆ free
- ☆ hopeful
- ☆ patient

- ☆ important
- ☆ valued
- ☆ fully realized
- ☆ valuable
- ☆ needed
- ☆ accepted
- ☆ honored
- ☆ treasured
- ☆ cherished
- ☆ worthwhile
- ☆ worthy
- ☆ fully qualified
- ☆ surrounded
- ☆ loved
- ☆ lovable
- ☆ not silent
- ☆ worth pursuing
- ☆ peaceful
- ☆ beautiful
- ☆ strong
- ☆ graceful
- ☆ compassionate
- ☆ thankful

- ☆ a princess/prince
- ☆ a warrior
- ☆ a king/queen
- ☆ an overcomer
- ☆ an heir
- ☆ royalty
- ☆ gentle
- ☆ wise
- ☆ appreciated
- ☆ smart
- ☆ generous
- ☆ courageous
- ☆ brave
- ☆ faithful
- ☆ loyal
- ☆ joyful
- ☆ forgiven
- ☆ honoring
- ☆ truthful
- ☆ honest
- ☆ dynamic
- ☆ godly
- ☆ righteous

My Outward Expressions

I am _____

I believe I am _____

Relationships closest to my heart:

My favorites:

toy growing up _____

spice _____

food _____

drink _____

book _____

movie _____

TV show _____

sport _____

hobby _____

color _____

item of clothing _____

How I like my eggs _____

Things in my pocket:

Places I've been:

I can _____

I will _____

My dreams / goals:

My self portrait:

My life verse:

My Inward Expressions

As the Lord reveals the truth of who you are, of how He sees you, record it on this page.

As the Lord shows you the truth of who He is, record it on this page.

My Declaration

Write your declaration of God's truth of who He created you to be as revealed throughout the course of your healing journey to this point. Review the pages of this journal, where you poured out your heart and the Father poured His heart into you, to remind yourself of these truths. Post this page in a place where you will see it often, and speak its words of truth over yourself daily.

_____
_____
_____
_____
_____
_____
_____
_____
_____
_____
_____
_____
_____
_____
_____
_____
_____
_____
_____
_____

My Healing Testimony

If you wish to give feedback or share your healing testimony, please fill out this page, snap a picture of it, and email it to <u>jdrozda@myaccess.ca</u>. Feel free to share any significant journal pages!

Comments: _____

_____

_____

_____

_____

_____

_____

My healing testimony

_____

_____

_____

_____

_____

_____

_____

_____

_____

_____

Prophetic Voices

Jeff Barnhardt
Evangelist, Event Speaker, Prophetic Leadership Team Member
Author of *God of Miracles: Ordinary People Extraordinary Stories* and
Destined to Be: Nine Keys to Live a Life of Purpose while Unlocking Your Full Potential
Contact - www.jeffbarnhardt.com

Kimm Reid
BAPsych, Co-founder of Ahelia Publishing, Children's Pastor
Fiction author of *Solstice Gates Series, Mercy Redeemed, Hadassah Unveiled, Nasha Uncovered* and non-fiction books: *Realigned:Bringing God's Promises from Heaven to Earth* and *Life Laid Down: Daring to Live Unordinary, Unstoppable, Unlimited.*
Event Speaker
Contact - kimm.reid@outlook.com

Maryann Ward
Author/Illustrator of *Olivia & Me*
Event Speaker
Contact - maryann@maward.ca

Val Byrd
Care, Connections, and Worship Pastor at Church of the Rock Calgary
Pastoral Mentor in Life Links
Seminar and Conference Speaker
Contact - val.k.byrd@gmail.com

Endnotes

[1] Michael Dye. *The Genesis Process.* https://www.genesisprocess.org (accessed December 10, 2017)

[2] Henderson, Robert. *Operating in the Courts of Heaven.* Shippensburg: Destiny Image, 2016.

[3] Roth, Sid. *It's Supernatural.* https://m.youtube.com (accessed December 8, 2017).

[4] Strauss, Jeanette. *From the Courtroom of Heaven To the Throne of Grace and Mercy.* Bradenton: Glorious Creations Publishing, 2011.

[5] Joyner, Rick. *The Final Quest.* Fort Mill: Morning Star Publications, 1996. p 123.

Acknowledgments

In the writing of this guide, I would like to acknowledge from where my help comes—God, my good Father, Jesus, my Redeemer, and Holy Spirit, my Teacher and constant Companion. It is all from You, for You; for Your glory.

Thank you to the creators of The Genesis Process, Elijah House, and The Cleansing Stream Ministries. As I have wrestled my way through my healing within your borders and continued on with training from your collective wisdom, it has become a part of me, and I am sure it flows throughout this guide.

I would also like to acknowledge all those who have walked alongside me somewhere along my path, playing big parts and little parts—but all significant—right from my first friend across the street, to those with whom I now link shields—my friends, colleagues, counselors, cheerleaders, and unofficial mentors, named and unnamed. I am so thankful you were and are all a part of my journey. You have made it beautiful, each in your own heartfelt way.

Debbie. Brenda G, Val & Halina. Margie, Ann & Diane. Christy, Darla, Kathy, Cathy, Brent & Brenda B, Cheryl, Maureen. Colleen, Bonnie & Wayne. Jeff & Brenda. Teena. Chandelle. Vickie, Carolyn & Dave, Lorna & Luis. Carmen. Alison S., Alison E., Suzanne, Paula, Jacqui, Barb, Merridy & Monica. Amanda & Tracy. Joylene. Lydia. Colleen. Christina. Ruebi. Dave and Linda & Joel and Ang. Jill and the Lisas. My soccer and basketball teams. Tara & Theresa. Jerri & Brett, Lillian. Allison & Rob. Pixie and Graham. Glen, Tracy, Kate & Alden and the Cleansing Stream Team. My Life Group. Theresa, Deb & Laura. Dorthy. Diane &Todd & Kathleen. Val & Ian. Jeff & Andrea. Kimm. Heather.

Between you all I have been inspired, helped, encouraged, believed in, corrected, taught, held up, picked up, counseled, loved, protected, cared for, and comforted. I thank all the others as well, impossible to name, who colored my world along the way.

I thank you, Kimm, my three-legged race partner—so very grateful God has put you with me in this race, so we could jump together into the realm of the impossible—the place where the Lord works best! Jarrod & Danielle, I am so so proud to call you mine. God has an amazing plan for you both. You will definitely use all the wisdom He is giving you. To my family and extended family—there are no words that can adequately describe the love and support you have given me as I had walked through the storms that were so frequent in my life. You have picked up so many pieces of me for so long. You are my heroes. I am excited that all of us now can see where those pieces belong; and that God has made something beautiful out of the messiness. Love you!

Allison, Kimm, Michele, Lorna, Pixie, Heather, Lillian & Jerahlyn—you go before me. You come behind me. You surround me. It has been an honor to walk with you in this journey.

What People are Saying about Invisible No More:

- This manual is like a hammer and chisel, used to chip away at the walls and barricades that people have built around themselves. As you begin reading this manual, I believe it will cause a shift in your heart. Those walls and barricades will become unstable—resulting in them being shattered and knocked down, enabling you to walk in your God-given identity. The blinders will be removed and you will have a greater vision of who you are in Christ. It is time for people to become unhidden; to shine and become all God has intended. I believe as a result of this, many, many leaders and world changers will rise up and begin to take the world by storm for Kingdom purposes. There is going to be a return to holiness and righteousness because of this manual and I believe we will begin to see a shift in society, to one that welcomes the presence of the Almighty Father.

Glenn Paguyo
Prophetic Leadership Team Member
Deliverance Ministry Leadership Team Member
Harvest City Church, Canada

- Despite being a Christian for 32 years, God continues to peel back layers, shedding light on issues that have kept me bound, impeding my walk and my witness. Recently, through the reading of Jocelyn Drozda's manual, *Invisible No More,* I've uncovered idols I had been unknowingly serving and recognized that I had a shame-based identity. We can only be healed when we realize and admit our need for healing and this guide helped to pinpoint various areas that had previously been hidden, such as lies I'd believed about myself and vows I'd made. I began to see how the enemy takes our giftings and distorts them, but that God's plan is to redeem those giftings, using them for His purposes, to bring Him glory. One powerful discovery was *Grieving Things Lost*. Before reading this section of the manual, I didn't realize I was still grieving deeply about various areas of my life, but as I began identifying and surrendering these things to God, I was overcome with emotion. When I began to write things down under the part, *Listening to the Lord*, the word "wallowing" jumped into my head. The dictionary definition of wallowing is "deliberately unhappy." I realized the lie I was believing was that I "deserved" to be unhappy because I was such a lousy mother, wife, Christian, and friend. I broke that lie off and aligned myself with truth. God knows the things I've said and done that weren't His heart, but He also knows my heart and that my intentions have always been good. He's been working on me in the areas of my weakness, but I needed to stop partnering with that lie. I would encourage all those who desire more freedom, peace, joy, and victory in their lives to pick up a copy of this Holy Spirit inspired manual and dive right in! Only God knows what you'll discover!

Michele Hastings
Educational Assistant

- Jocelyn opens the pages of her own journal, giving us a glimpse of how twisted lies, false beliefs, and inner vows attempt to sabotage and govern our beliefs and feelings. Jocelyn invites us into a process of journaling and collaborating with Holy Spirit as we explore, expose, confront, forgive, repent, surrender, grieve, heal, declare God's truth, and find identity in Him. Unbeknown to me, God set me up when Jocelyn asked if I would read and journal the first chapters of the manual. I agreed, not realizing God had something big ahead for me. Like Jocelyn, I have been on a healing journey for a long time, but recently Holy Spirit spoke into my spirit in a deeper, wider, and higher way than ever before. God told me He created me to love and be loved. Recently, a prophetic word was spoken over me; Love, Love, Love. An inner resolve has come over me; strength and purpose has become evident to others and me. Holy Spirit has anointed and directed Jocelyn to pen His Words; words, I was unaware were restoring confidence, widening my sphere of influence, and aligning me with God's truth and purposes. I am confident Holy Spirit will continue to use this manual in the lives of many. Look for His truth and declarations at the end of each chapter, and step confidently into the process of finding your identity in Christ Jesus. Thanks Jocelyn, for your obedience to Holy Spirit and thanks Jesus, for always interceding on my behalf.

Karen Paterson
EAL Educational Assistant
Deliverance Ministry Intercessory Team

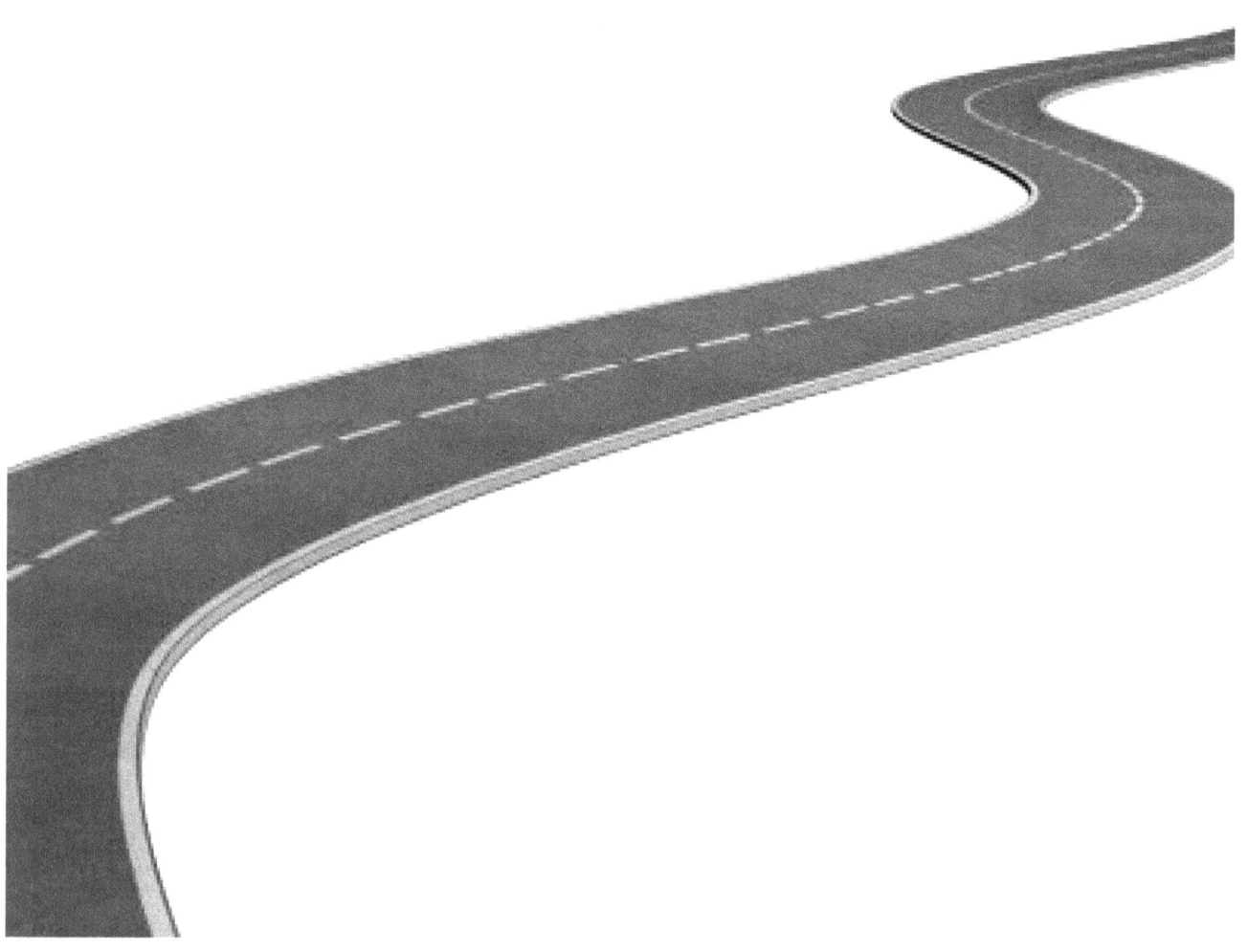

Book Two
Personal Identity Restored

Book Two—Personal Identity Restored

    Unit One—Walking Through the Pain (Coping Mechanisms)

    Unit Two—The Disappearing Act (Self-Hatred)

    Unit Three—The Breach-Wall (Fear)

    Unit Four—Expectancy (Surrender)

    Unit Five—Treasure Hunt (Buried Hopes)

    Unit Six—The Question of Sexuality (Sexuality and Gender)

    Unit Seven—The Enemy's Bitter Fruit (Depression, Anxiety ...)

www.ingramcontent.com/pod-product-compliance
Lightning Source LLC
Chambersburg PA
CBHW081458070526
44586CB00019B/2405